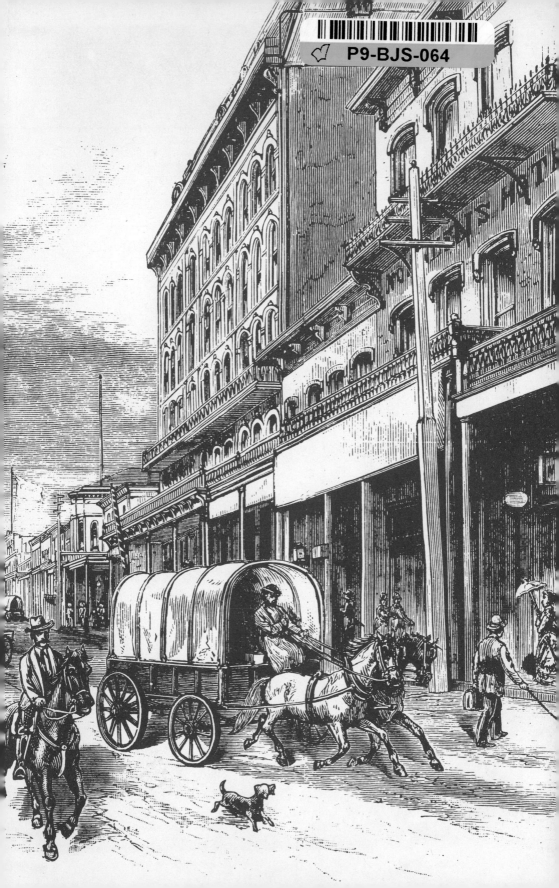

Books by LUCIUS BEEBE and CHARLES CLEGG

Highball, A Railroad Pageant

Mixed Train Daily

U.S. West, The Saga of Wells Fargo

Virginia & Truckee

*Legends of the Comstock Lode**

Cable Car Carnival

Hear the Train Blow

Books by LUCIUS BEEBE

High Iron, A Book of Trains

Highliners, A Railroad Album

Trains in Transition

Boston and the Boston Legend

Snoot If You Must

The Stork Club Bar Book

Comstock Commotion, The Story of
THE TERRITORIAL ENTERPRISE*

* Available from Stanford University Press.

COMSTOCK COMMOTION

COMSTOCK

STANFORD UNIVERSITY PRESS

COMMOTION

THE STORY OF

THE

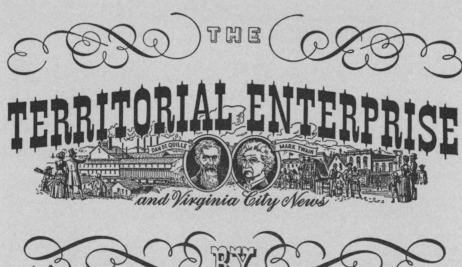

TERRITORIAL ENTERPRISE

and Virginia City News

BY

LUCIUS BEEBE

STANFORD, CALIFORNIA

ACKNOWLEDGMENTS

For their many good and gracious offices in assisting in the preparation of the story of THE TERRITORIAL ENTERPRISE, the author wishes
to convey his most distinguished thanks to John Barr Tompkins of
the research staff of the Bancroft Library at Berkeley, to Joe Farns-
worth, formerly Nevada State Printer at Carson City, to Professor
A. L. Higginbotham of the University of Nevada, to Sinclair Ross of
Volcano, California, for the design of the title page, to Phil Townsend
Hanna, a student of THE ENTERPRISE legend, to Dr. Effie Mona Mack,
from whose works much source material was secured, to Thomas C.
Wilson for permission to reproduce art work belonging to Harold's
Club of Reno, to Mrs. Clara Beatty of the Nevada State Historical
Society, and to Irene Simpson of the History Room at the Wells Fargo
Bank & Union Trust Company in San Francisco.

STANFORD UNIVERSITY PRESS, STANFORD, CALIFORNIA

Published in Great Britain, India, and Pakistan by Geoffrey Cumberlege,
Oxford University Press, London, Bombay, and Karachi

The Baker and Taylor Company, Hillside, New Jersey
Henry M. Snyder & Company, Inc., 440 Fourth Avenue, New York 16
W. S. Hall & Company, 457 Madison Avenue, New York 22

TABLE OF CONTENTS

JOHN & LAREE CAUGHEY

The Title Page illustration, depicting a cheerful moment in the daily life of The Enterprise, *is posed against a background of the Enterprise Building erected in 1863 and still occupied by the publication. On the Table of Contents page a similar interlude is depicted before the paper's second premises in North C Street, briefly occupied in 1861 and '62.*

A Paper Is Born

IN THE very shadow of the High Sierra, in a drafty shack through whose chinks the December snowfall filtered to form miniature drifts along floor and windowsill, two bearded men assisted by an apprentice boy wrestled with a secondhand Washington printing press.

The patent furniture of the primeval instrument was cold. So were the chases holding the long columns of agate and brevier in at least an approximation of true alignment. The ink on the hand-activated inking roller had forgotten that it was ever fluid. Everything was gelid to the touch and the breath of the two frock-coated men turned white as they panted over their task. The cannon-ball stove in the corner, for all it glowed red with a fire of cottonwood logs, hardly made a dent in the antarctic cold that enveloped the entire Territory of Western Utah.

The two men made frequent reference to a handy black bottle containing a sovereign remedy of the countryside, called valley tan; and the apprentice boy made mental notes to explore some day for himself its possibilities.

The two ancients also cursed with fearful and ornate profanity, drawing upon resources of the literary antiquities both Biblical and profane, upon the classical humanities, upon the Book of Mormon, and upon a surprising knowledge of anatomic possibilities both animal and human. They cursed Nevada by sections and quarter sections. And most of all they made special reservations in the permanent residential areas of hell for Richard M. Hoe, in far-off New York, who had devised the infernal contrivance with which they were contesting, and his brother Robert Hoe, who merchandised the artifact.

The accursed brothers Hoe conducted a well-established and highly profitable business in downtown Manhattan at the corner of Broome and Sheriff streets, where they offered for sale all sorts of ingenious aids to printing: hand presses of the Washington plan, proofing machines, stitching and binding devices, type cases and such. But only hell itself, the two printers of Mormon Station were in accord, could have outshopped such a desperate devising as the one at hand; and back to the foundries and machine shops of hell they consigned the Hoes and all their works.

The elder and more proficient blasphemer, did he but know it, was merely getting in practice for an exercise in cursing some twenty years later which would become legendary throughout the entire West and elevate the technique of execration to realms of supernal artistry.

In desperation, the thwarted molders of the public mind poured Niagaras of valley tan into themselves and over the running parts of the machinery as a lubricant. Wasn't it an accepted fact that whisky was in the ink of the pioneer press both metaphorically and factually? And at length the machinery creaked into a reasonable facsimile of action, and the more sober partner was able to snatch from its inner economy the six-column one sheet—the first copy of the first newspaper ever to be printed in the howling wilderness of Nevada.

The logotype read, THE TERRITORIAL ENTERPRISE.

Thus, in a mist both blasphemous and alcoholic, prophetic of things to come, was born the paper that was shortly to be the pattern and glass of frontier journalism everywhere, and eventually was to achieve immortality as one of the romantic properties of the Old American West.

Lacking the crystal ball of Mrs. Sandy Bowers, a seeress even at that moment headed for the same place as THE ENTERPRISE, thirty miles distant on the slopes of Mount Davidson, W. L. Jernegan and Alfred James were unable to see the promise of things to come in their so perilously delivered child. The partners buttoned their frock coats across their chests against the elements and ran through the snow to the Stockade Bar to show the first copy of the paper to Isaac Roop, who happened to be in town from Susanville.

Other than the indomitable hanker of the frontier to set itself up in the pattern of the good life the pioneers had known back home, it is difficult at this remove to understand what motivated the seedy itinerants Jernegan and James to ferry Nevada's first newspaper bodily overland from Salt Lake by ox team and hang out their shingle in Mormon Station. The community, which was later to change its name to Genoa, as it remains to this day, numbered something fewer than two hundred permanent residents. It was a freighting station on the emigrant route to California, a staging depot where teamsters and draymen changed horses and oxen for the ascent of the Sierra on the way to Lake Tahoe, Strawberry, Sportsman's Hall, and, eventually, Hangtown.

Mormon Station needed a newspaper far less than it required a physician, a pharmacist, and an undertaker. It had a sufficiency of wheelwrights, farriers, and bartenders. A newspaper was at best a devising of metropolitan luxury; at worst, an economic folly. But just as every community in the land must, only a few years from now, have a railroad of its very own, so did every hamlet and crossroads in the West pant as the hart panteth for the water springs for its own newspaper. Jernegan and James were the men anointed to bring this consummation to Mormon Station on the evening of December 18, 1858.

Save by professional chroniclers of yesterday, Jernegan and James are forgotten now, but once, like the stout Cortez, they stood on a peak in Darien and a world spread itself before them. They were the prototype and archetype of the frontier printer, in soup-stained frock coat and dented top hat, resolute, his breath perfumed with strong waters, type stick in one hand, the other on the stock of a belted gun, facing Indians, the wilderness, the opposition, creditors, and hangover. O Pioneers!

Jernegan and James, according to Dan De Quille in later years, had been at something of a loss for a name for their paper and had written to a friend in the Mother Lode diggings of California, one Washington Wright, asking for suggestions. A return letter from Wright, brought to Mormon Station by Snowshoe Thompson, the universal postman, suggested that since the venture was a new enterprise in the then Territory of Western Utah, what could be more appropriate than THE TERRITORIAL ENTERPRISE?

Jernegan and James were delighted and invited everyone in the Stockade Bar to have something for their stomachs, and THE ENTERPRISE became the first of many papers of that name elsewhere in the land.

No self-respecting newspaper in those mannered days could come into being without a prospectus, and the partners lost no time in having one run up. It read:

A JOURNAL FOR THE EASTERN SLOPE

The Undersigned very respectfully announce that they will commence on the first week of November next, 1858, at Carson City, Eagle Valley, the publication of a Weekly Independent Newspaper, entitled *The Territorial Enterprise*. It will industriously and earnestly be devoted to the advancement of everything pertaining to the beautiful country bounded on the West by the Sierra Nevadas and extending into and forming the Great Basin of the Continent. . . . The arrivals and departures of the Great Overland Mail and the incidents thereto will be carefully noted, and it will be the aim and pride of the undersigned to print a Journal which will be popular with and advantageous to every resident of the Utah Valleys. They, therefore, confidently rely upon the encouragement and liberality of their fellow residents.

W. L. JERNEGAN & ALFRED JAMES

The first issue of THE ENTERPRISE appeared neither at Carson City nor during the first week of November.

For reasons which have not survived, the proprietors decided on Mormon Station, perhaps because while all the teaming headed for the Sierra passes went through there it did not all go through Carson, a deal of it deriving from Carson Valley without passing through the future state capital itself. The postponement of the first issue was ascribable to mechanical breakdown.

At the last moment it was discovered that the publishers were shy of type. There were insufficient characters of a given face to piece out cross-heads and display lines, and an urgent note was dispatched by Snowshoe Thompson to a Hangtown dealer in such matters, begging a shirttail of metal on loan and promising to repay in the terms of optimism customary in such crises. All the stage roads were already blockaded by snow and the drivers and teamsters securely holed up in Mormon Station for a winter of draw poker and Saturday night stabbings, so the precious type had to come back in the pack of the irreplaceable Snowshoe.

No copy of that historic first paper has survived into the present, although its front page is reproduced in the then new halftone process in Thompson & West's monumental history of Nevada. The mortality rate among early Western documents in an age of wooden buildings and universal conflagration was fearfully high.

The front-page date line of THE ENTERPRISE in its earliest issues read "Carson Valley, Utah Territory—Published Every Saturday Morning at the Office on Mill Street, Genoa, Carson Valley."

The copy for July 30, 1859, which reached the hands of Thompson & West and has since disappeared from human ken, was devoted in its entirety to printing the proceedings of the Constitutional Convention which had convened at Genoa twelve days earlier.

Knowing the sources of contemporary news, however, it is easy to reconstruct in the mind's eye the early issues of the paper. Notices of jury duty were flanked by advertisements for Stoughton's Bitters. Proclamations by Isaac Roop, by now governor, ran next to the notices of sales by Mormon farmers relinquishing reluctantly their rich farmsteads along the valleys of Western Utah to answer the recall to Deseret. There were the births and deaths of a community of two hundred pioneers, the departures of the great Overland Stages for Sacramento and Salt Lake, disquieting stories of Indians along the Humboldt and, as the year 1859 drew to a close, squibs telling with increasing frequency of the discoveries of gold along the slopes of Mount Davidson thirty-odd miles to the north.

Matters of national consequence arrived in the form of news boldly lifted without so much as by-your-leave, as was the universal custom of the time, from six-weeks-old copies of the bedsheet-size *Boston Advertiser*, the *National Intelligencer* from Washington, the weekly edition of Horace Greeley's revered *New York Tribune*, and the *New Orleans Picayune*, the nation's leading journals of news and opinion of the era.

The winter of 1859 was rough. Snows up to 100 inches fell on the level, and drifts of incalculable depth blocked the high passes of the Sierra. Twice the paper stock of THE ENTERPRISE ran out and the partners were unable to find newsprint to meet their publication date, with the result that at the end of their first year their volume was incomplete by six papers. Other frontier papers in this situation sometimes printed a few token sheets, just to maintain continuity, on wallpaper or butcher's wrapping stock, but even these last recourses were not available in Mormon Station. Jernegan and James buttoned their frock coats tighter, absorbed heroic quantities of valley tan, and resumed publication when Snowshoe Thompson came over the hill with a few precious sheets of newsprint from the dealer in Hangtown.

It was all in the accepted scheme of things for pioneer editors.

So were occasional short rations.

Both during its stay in Carson and Eagle valleys, as well as during its early existence on the Comstock, THE ENTERPRISE' editors sometimes fell upon lean days. Hard currency was difficult to come by and credit more so. Often subscribers paid in trade goods and if half a bear, a hind quarter of venison, or a dozen sage hens arrived in payment of the delinquent subscription, the staff lived high as long as the fat of the land lasted. "Let us indulge our vanity by saying that we yield to none as a caterer to the inner man," wrote Jernegan at the time, "whatever our shortcomings in regard to intellectual pabulum."

THE TERRITORIAL ENTERPRISE, destined to occupy many premises in the next ninety-five years of its existence, first published, so far as can be ascertained, from a still standing, one-story wooden shack on the northern outskirts of Mormon Station, but shortly thereafter occupied quarters in Singleton's Hall, the Nevada Hotel, "a room indiscriminately used by preachers, debating clubs, and secret societies." Mormon Station had no jail at the time and, on one eventful occasion, a prisoner awaiting trial was chained to the Washington hand press with a logging chain for three days.

PRIMAL PRESS FOR A PRIMEVAL NEWSPAPER

THE PRESS on which the first issue of THE TERRITORIAL ENTERPRISE was printed in Christmas week of 1858 was the so-called "acorn" model of Hoe's Washington hand press, its name deriving from the shape of its frame. Balky, and by some printers termed downright vindictive, it still turned out a print job far superior to that of many later power-operated presses.

IN THIS RUDE SHACK still standing at Genoa, Nevada, THE ENTERPRISE first saw the light of day and several issues were printed here before the proprietors removed to Singleton's Hall, a premises more proof against the elemental winters of Nevada Territory.

A PAPER IS BORN

But all through the terrible winter of '59, destiny was hovering uncertainly above the snowdrifts of Gold Canyon, which led up a five-mile-long ravine from Carson Water at Dayton to a point halfway up the precipitous side of Mount Davidson overlooking the old Emigrant Trail to California and, in the distance, the Sink of Carson and the blue mountains of the Reese River.

For a full decade, ever since the first overland covered wagons had passed along Carson Water on the way to El Dorado in the Mother Lode, pocket gold had been turned up on the slopes of the Washoe hills by casual prospectors. It wasn't much, and only a few easily discouraged pilgrims, dismayed by the prospect of one more mountain range to cross, had settled down on the eastern slope of the Sierra; the little crossroads town of Dayton, where they had to make up their minds whether to stay in Utah Territory or pass over into California, was for a time and locally known as Pause-and-Ponder.

Ten-dollar bonanzas in Gold Canyon kept turning up just regularly enough to keep the Washoe prospectors in beans and whisky. The overture to the great first movement of what was shortly to be a crashing symphony of riotous riches was being played as no more than a refrain of distant woodwinds and muted French horns half heard above the wind in the sagebrush.

Comers to the scene who had made their exeunt where none might follow had been the brothers Ethan and Hosea Grosch, sons of a Utica clergyman back in upper York State, who had intimatings of bonanzas to come but whose secret had perished with them in the rigors of the Nevada winter. Part possessor of stolen knowledge of the Grosches was Henry Comstock, a windy no-gooder who had watched the comings and goings of the brothers as they worked a tenacious blue clay in their crude rockers. Neighboring no-gooder and a human wine cellar to boot was James Finney, alias "Old Virginny," who was on the lam from a California sheriff for a sordid and by now all but forgotten knifing up Downieville way. Farther up Gold Canyon operated a disreputable partnership of musical comedy Irishmen dressed to make an entry into history with short-stemmed clay pipes and silk top hats without brims. Peter O'Riley and Pat McLaughlin were amiable no-gooders, as honest as might be but not right bright in the head and easily imposed on when the time came round, which was to be very shortly.

Stray echoes of these things drifted down the wind and eventually became record in the columns of THE TERRITORIAL ENTERPRISE at Mormon Station.

7

COMSTOCK COMMOTION

One night Old Virginny Finney and Old Pancake Comstock became uncommonly drunk in the shack town near the head of Gold Canyon. Their footing was unsteady, their wolf calls and Dionysiac tumult frightened the wild life of Mount Davidson. Suddenly, unimaginable catastrophe struck. While attempting the mere elementary routine of smashing the neck of a whisky bottle against a rock to provide easy access to its content, Old Virginny lost his expertise and shattered the entire bottle.

Only for a moment was he paralyzed with horror; then man's godlike capacity for rising above disaster asserted itself and Old Virginny screamed: "I christen this place Virginia City." He had named a place for himself anyway.

Neither Old Virginny Finney nor Old Pancake Comstock had any idea of the sort of place it was going to be.

Ho For Washoe!

THE RUSH to the new diggings of Washoe, of which Virginia City was the metropolis, gathered momentum throughout 1859, and W. L. Jernegan and Alfred James began to gaze longingly across the lush (but after all only agricultural) meadows of Carson Valley, to where Mount Davidson loomed against the horizon, with God only knew what bonanzas being discovered daily on its barren slopes.

An assay from the mound of red earth later to be known as Gold Hill had been carried across the Sierra in the inevitable pack of Snowshoe Thompson and showed $2,200 a ton in gold by a Sacramento assayer. Pete O'Riley and Pat McLaughlin were sometimes taking as much as $200 in pure dust from their rockers at the close of the working day, and Old Pancake Comstock, a muscle man at heart, had cut himself in on the claims of the gullible Gaels with seemingly convincing evidence of prior ownership.

The Mormon lady named Eilley Orrum, lately quit of one husband and now rejoicing in another, Sandy Bowers, packed her boardinghouse on a wagon, provided passage on mule back for her two star boarders, Jim Rogers and Joe Plato, and moved up-canyon to be near the scene of everything exciting.

The region was producing so much wealth, sometimes as much as $500 a day, that Old Pancake was almost constantly in wine and spoke grandly of the ore body underfoot as the Comstock Lode. Virginia City on the Comstock Lode, for all it represented thirty authentic tent residences and six packing cases with holes cut in them for doors, had a satisfying sound that was grateful to Old Virginny and Old Pancake alike.

There was no telling where this sort of thing might end. Perhaps one of these days the Great Overland Staging Company would pause for mail at the foot of Gold Canyon on its weekly excursions across a continent— just a soap box on a post, of course, for messages; no attendant or stables, since these were close at hand at Fort Churchill. But the Comstock and Virginia City were growing. Everyone said so.

By the autumn of 1859, W. L. Jernegan and Alfred James could stand

9

it in Mormon Station no longer. Everyone in Carson Valley had taken off for the Washoe diggings as soon as the hay was in, and life in Carson City, where Major William M. Ormsby had erected a two-story adobe handy to the Plaza, was becoming consequential.

Moving a newspaper in those halcyon times was no major effort. Itinerant printers roamed up and down the country with all the resources for setting up a metropolitan press in a two-wheeled oxcart. In most cases the name of the weekly was changed with its location and to suit its new base of operations, but THE TERRITORIAL ENTERPRISE didn't even have to do that. Its logotype was valid anywhere from Great Salt Lake to the shores of Lake Bigler, as Tahoe was then known.

On Saturday, October 29, 1859, THE TERRITORIAL ENTERPRISE ran its final paper under the Mormon Station date line. In the past few months the place had changed its name to Genoa and that was bad luck, too. A good place to leave. So a wagon backed up to Singleton's Hall, the Nevada Hotel, and the territory's first newspaper, press, type cases, paper cutter, spittoons, the office revolver, a deer's-horn hatrack, six tall stools, and a steel engraving of Gray's Dragoons charging the Mexican cannon at Resaca de la Palma were loaded aboard and started up the valley road toward Carson.

The journey itself consumed less than a single day but, while setting down the load in front of Major Ormsby's adobe, pilgrim feet became tangled and a type case containing twenty trays of pearl and pica went onto the sidewalk in a hideous pi. The delay, as it turned out, lasted for almost a year.

Nobody could have been more pleased with this typographical contretemps than Abraham V. Z. Curry, who had himself shaken the dust of Mormon Station from his teamster's boots early in the year and departed in one of the greatest huffs in Nevada history.

Able Abe was one of the first refugees from California. He had seen the elephant in the Mother Lode and wasn't impressed. Besides, all available townsites in that part of the world had been bought up and were being exploited by realtors who were plainly extortionists, and the dream of Abe's life was to found, develop, and expand a town of his very own. It didn't have to be called Currytown or Abe's Corners, he wasn't vain that way, but it was damn well going to be known everywhere as Abe Curry's town and he was going to be the boss man in it.

Abe's acquisitive eye had already lighted on Mormon Station as the possible instrument of his landed ambitions, but a real estate speculator there, who had plainly been to California and learned the technique of the land swindle from masters, tried to sell him a lot in the Nevada desert with a hundred-foot frontage for a cool $1,000. Abe had blistered the ears of everyone within hearing with a choice selection of prose picked up in Negro Bar and Whisky Flat and had platted a township all his own fifteen miles up the road, calling it Carson in honor of whom do you suppose who was a mighty pathfinder and powerful killer of Indians? Abe hated Indians and named his town for Kit.

The only business on the site of the future capital when Abe arrived dreaming chamber-of-commerce dreams was the Eagle Trading Post and store, conducting a very good business right on the Emigrant Trail where it began the ascent of King's Canyon Grade to the Sierra ramparts. Frank Bernard and George Follansbee, who owned the Eagle, saw eye to eye with Abe; a surveyor was imported on the first down stage from Dayton, and Curry was well started on his project to bust the land pirates of Mormon Station as high as a kite on the Fourth of July.

Fortune, who may well have overheard Abe's board-of-trade sales talk, promptly dealt the old gentleman a full hand. First of all, a frivolous acquaintance was in the habit of saluting him as colonel and the title stuck. Abe became Colonel Curry and the advancement raised the tone of the entire community. Then came the Comstock boom just a spell up the trail, and by the time Virginia City was a proven diggings its fortunes were reflected in an interlocking boom in freighting and miners' supplies in Carson City.

Wells Fargo & Co. established a branch office there and Carson was a made town, its future in the bag. The presence of Wells Fargo was a hallmark of the established community everywhere and the arrival of one of the all-powerful firm's route agents and local managers was the equivalent of that of a full ambassador in other parts of the world.

When it was apparent to everyone that business was being drained away from Mormon Station and that Carson was growing fat on its rival's misfortunes, the colonel's cup was running over. All he needed was a newspaper, and what was that coming up the road in an oxcart guided by two drunken printers?

THE TERRITORIAL ENTERPRISE, of course.

The providential piing of its type was pure anticlimax so far as Curry was concerned. He knew he was in a winning cycle and no good fortune would have surprised him.

"Things are looking up; we've got a newspaper!" the colonel remarked on encountering Captain Anton Tjader, late of the U.S. Navy, in the Plaza. The town was full of military titles.

"I heard some powerful swearing down in front of Major Ormsby's block," allowed the captain, "but didn't know what it was about. A newspaper, you say? Well, well!"

"The Territorial Enterprise," explained Curry grandly. "Couldn't stand the pukes down there in that cesspool of Mormon Station. Decided to do business in a white man's town. A newspaper can do a town like this a mort of good!"

"Could make a millionaire-man of its owner if it was run right," said the colonel reflectively.

The colonel and the captain stepped into the City Exchange Saloon for a snort.

Had he been aware that, so far as the management of The Enterprise was concerned, Carson City was only a way station, Colonel Curry's language can only be conjectured.

Quite aside from the matter of the pied type, however, Carson City possessed advantages that at once became apparent to the management of its unexpected newspaper. Three express and stage lines were in operation between Carson City and Sacramento, not counting the through services of the Great Overland line. One of them was the celebrated Pioneer Stage Company set up by the remarkable Louis McLane and his brother Charles which, in turn, connected with the vast freight and staging empire of Russell, Majors, & Waddell at Salt Lake. Due to the competition over the Sierra it was possible to send express letters to California for the nominal fee of two bits; and the Messrs. Jernegan and James, for a dollar, could have sent in enough papers from which to crib the news of the world to fill the columns of The Enterprise ten times over.

There was also in much admired operation the Placerville, Humboldt & Salt Lake Telegraph, which came into town, appropriately enough, right down Telegraph Street. The telegraph tariff was a little rich for the blood of The Enterprise and the management rudely refused to accept advertising space in lieu of cash. Jernegan and James gave their correspondence for California to the Pioneer and had the satisfaction of knowing that whenever one of McLane's stages broke a harness strap or loosened a tire up Strawberry way the driver merely appropriated a length of the telegraph company's copper wire which ran handily from tree to tree along the highway to make the repair. The service as a result could be described as intermittent.

Carson City during the year The Enterprise made its abode upstairs in Major Ormsby's adobe on the Plaza, while not a community which participated in sarabands of sin to elevate it to the status of other Western frontier towns like Dodge City, Newton, Tombstone, Last Chance Gulch, Julesburg, or the Cherry Creek Diggings, was wild enough to be a curtain raiser for the drama of Virginia City, in which THE ENTERPRISE was soon to be one of the starred performers. When the territorial legislature met a year or so later, one of its first acts took cognizance of "noisy and profane amusements on the first day of the week, commonly called the Lord's Day," and moved to abate them. It had no success.

The major excitement of THE ENTERPRISE' year in Carson City was the war between the settlers of Western Nevada and the Piute Indians, a series of more or less bloody skirmishes which threw the entire territory into panic and must have received top billing in the capital's first and for a time only newspaper.

Alas, that for this period the files of THE ENTERPRISE simply do not exist. Neither in the great Coe Collection of Western Americana at New Haven, or in the vaults of the Mackay School of Mines in Reno, nor among the treasures of the Bancroft Library at Berkeley is there a copy of THE TERRITORIAL ENTERPRISE bearing the date line of Carson City, Nevada Territory.

A single unique copy in the possession of today's owners of THE ENTERPRISE survives, but the date is December 17, 1859, and it contains no mention of the Piute troubles which had terrified the countryside the previous spring.

This first anniversary issue contains a review of the past year's achievement and gives thanks that the affairs of THE TERRITORIAL ENTERPRISE seem in a promising way at last. During the past winter the staff had suffered from lack of fuel and on several occasions had been forced to suspend for want of paper so that the anniversary issue is No. 45 instead of No. 51, but things are better now. The paper is comfortably lodged in Major Ormsby's adobe, the major himself having unhappily perished in the Piute campaigns. Mr. Jonathan Williams has become associated with the management and is even now in California attending, in a manner not specified, to the paper's affairs.

In common with the affairs of THE ENTERPRISE, Carson has expanded and waxed prosperous as the territorial capital. The Downieville Restaurant, Richard Stege proprietor, has moved its business bodily across the Sierra and become "a rendezvous for visitors to the New Diggings." Adolph Waitz, owner of the Carson City Hotel, is happy to announce that his

"Bedding & Table are superior to any that will be found on this side of The Mountains." The Nevada Hotel is newly furnished throughout and calls special attention to its bedding department, which cannot be excelled. With a new bakery attached to its premises, the Pioneer Hotel speaks for the quality and abundance of its table fare. Captain Anton Tjader, mentioned above in converse with Colonel Curry and late of the U.S. Marine Hospital, Chelsea, Massachusetts, offers his professional services, with gunshot wounds a specialty, and $25 reward is being offered for three boxes containing glasses, crucibles, etc., addressed to F. Horn, assayer at Virginia City, lost during the recent storm somewhere on the King's Canyon Grade.

"Carson in its early years was a decidedly free and independent community whose citizens did about as they pleased," says Jock Taylor, the town's historian, writing for THE ENTERPRISE in later years. If they wanted to sleep they slept, if they wanted to fight, they fought. Whatever they did was considered their own business. Even the girls were lively. The *State Register* casually mentions two who rode up Carson Street in an open sleigh, indulged in some form of disagreement, then stopped the sleigh in the middle of the street and got out and had a fistfight. Finally, their disagreement more or less adjusted, they got in and rode off together, "leaving much of their outer clothing and many ribbons behind."

Forethoughtful Colonel Curry, co-owner of everything in sight, had erected his Hot Springs Hotel at Carson Warm Springs, later to be the site of the state penitentiary, and when the first legislature convened lacking any place of assembly, he offered the unused third story of his hostel to the homeless solons. To accommodate them on the two-mile trip out from Carson City he built Nevada's first railroad, a tramline powered by mules over which a springless streetcar ferried the lawgivers to and from legislative session. The Eagle Valley Railroad was not entirely philanthropic. Over it from the quarries at Warm Springs moved profitable loads of dressed stone from which the first permanent buildings in Carson and later the state capitol itself were built.

A description of THE ENTERPRISE during its Carson interlude has been provided by the incomparable J. Ross Browne, who paused there briefly on the first of his two memorable trips to the Comstock as staff reporter and sketch artist for *Harper's Monthly*. Even in its infancy the paper was becoming a legend in the West.

Chief among the curiosities of Carson City [wrote Browne] is *The Territorial Enterprise*, a newspaper of an origin anterior to the mining excitement. I was introduced to "the Colonel" who presides over the editorial department

LITERARY TEA

WHEN J. ROSS BROWNE visited Western Nevada for the first time in 1859 to report its already legendary bonanzas for *Harper's Weekly*, he stopped off at Carson City on his way to Washoe to pay a professional call on the management of THE TERRITORIAL ENTERPRISE, and his account of its personnel and premises is one of the first extant records of the paper's early days. Browne's subsequent report on the prospects of the Comstock was not altogether in keeping with Virginia City's optimistic view of the future, and when Browne revisited Nevada four years later he anticipated his possible reception in this humorous sketch which ran in *Harper's* with the caption: "The Author's Reception at Virginia City." Actually he was met by a delegation from his old friends on THE ENTERPRISE and escorted with every hospitable attention to the Howling Wilderness Saloon. A man, especially a newspaperman, could work up a powerful thirst on the long ride from Strawberry Station.

and found him uncommonly strong in the ultimate destiny of Carson. His office was located in a dirty frame shanty, and general rubbish of dark and literary aspect; there those astounding editorials which now and then arouse the public mind are concocted. The Colonel and his compositors live in a sort of family fashion, entirely free from the rigorous etiquette of such establishments in New York. They cook their own food in the composing room (which is also the editorial and press room) and being, as a general thing, short of plates, use the frying pan in common for that purpose. In cases of great festivity and rejoicing, when a subscriber has settled up arrears or the cash is paid down for a good job of hand-bills, the Colonel purchases the best tenderloin steak to be had in the market, cooks it with one hand while with the other he writes a letter of thanks to the subscriber or a puff on the hand-bill.

Browne's homely picture of life on a pioneer newspaper might have been written with only a degree of variation of scores of shops, where the intimate chronicle of the Old West, quite divorced of implications of continental destinies, was written by seedy Plutarchs whose frock coats were green with age and whose hands quivered with drunkard's palsy.

Just what it was that, as THE ENTERPRISE' stay in Carson City was drawing to a close, disenchanted W. L. Jernegan and Alfred James must forever be a mystery. Perhaps they shared the heresy, openly expressed at various times in all mining camps, that the Comstock bonanzas were worked out, had been merely surface outcroppings whose cream had been skimmed, and that the camp was headed back to the sagebrush oblivion from which it had emerged with such gaudy hooray.

Perhaps some incompatibility arose between the partners. No one will ever know.

On the very threshold of the effulgent sunrise of its fortunes, THE TERRITORIAL ENTERPRISE was sold. A succession of new owners briefly dominated the editorial rooms and mechanical departments in Major Ormsby's adobe. On Saturday, August 20, 1859, the James partnership was acquired by Jonathan Williams and the firm name changed to Jernegan & Co. A year later the paper appeared without Jernegan's name and listed Williams & Degroot as editors and proprietors. On September 29, 1860, Williams' name alone adorned the masthead and the new proprietor announced his intention at long last of resuming the interrupted *jornada* of THE ENTERPRISE from Mormon Station to Virginia City.

Thus the primal, elder father of Nevada journalism fades into the mists, to emerge but once again, and that twenty years later, and in an incandescent manner quite in keeping with the character of the property he had sired and spurned.

Territorial Enterprise.

CARSON CITY, NEVADA TERRITORY, SATURDAY, DECEMBER 17, 1859.

VOL. 1.   NO. 45.

Territorial Enterprise.

Published every Saturday morning, at the Office on Carson st., between 2d and 3d, up stairs, Carson City, Nevada Territory.

—BY—

W. L. JERNEGAN & CO.

Terms,—Invariably in Advance,

One Year	$5 00.
Six Months	4 00.
Three Months	3 00..
Single Copies	25.

Advertising.

One Square, 10 lines, first insertion, $3—each subsequent insertion, $1 50. Business Cards of ten lines or less, one year, $25; three months, $10.

A liberal discount will be made on the above rates, for all yearly and quarterly advertisements which exceed one square.

Agents for the Enterprise:

THOMAS BOYCE	SAN FRANCISCO.
CHAS. A. CRANE	SAN FRANCISCO.
A. BADLAM & E. B. DAVIDSON	SACRAMENTO.
E. M. HILL	MARYSVILLE.
J. C. KERLEY	PLACERVILLE.
J. M. CLARK	COLOMA.
W. S. DAY	DIAMOND SPRINGS.
JOHN W. OREAR	DOWNIEVILLE.

Departure of Col. Musser.

Col. J. J. Musser, our recently elected Delegate to Congress, left for Washington, on business connected with the interests of Nevada Territory, on Monday morning last. Col. Musser bears with him the confidence, respect and hearty good will of our people. His abilities are undoubted, and his opportunities for earning a just fame are as fair as any now presented. He has reasons numerous and cogent to urge upon Congress, in favor of Nevada Territory. He possesses the requisite ability to present them properly; and if Congress fails to give us what we so much need, a separate organization, it will not be for want of energetic representation of our interests. We say, God speed! to Col. Musser. It will be a proud day for him, and for the residents of these Valleys, when he shall return with the Bill organizing the Territory of Nevada. And it will be a no less proud day for our

Ourselves.

One year ago to-day, the first number of the TERRITORIAL ENTERPRISE was issued at Genoa. Our publishing room was in Singleton's Hall, Nevada Hotel, a room indiscriminately used by preachers, debating-clubs, secret societies, and once at least, for a prison. Upon the latter occasion we had a man accused of crime chained to our printing press, with a log chain, for two days and a half. What secrets that old Hall might tell, could it, by chance, be endowed with the gift of speech! Our establishment was removed to Carson City, on Thursday, Nov. 10, 1859. We now occupy half of the upper part of Major Ormsby's adobe building, southwest corner of the Plaza. Our volume is not yet completed by seven numbers, owing to the fact that we have twice been compelled to suspend our issue for want of paper. During last winter, most of our paper was brought over on snow shoes, by attaches of this office. Many a time in the past year have we suffered for lack of fuel, and been pinched for want of actual necessaries of life. But so far as we have struggled on successfully, and to-day we find ourselves in more comfortable circumstances in many respects. To be sure we still have to descend from the editorial tripod to superintend the cooking of a beefsteak, the seasoning of a bean soup, or the concoction of a pot of coffee, (and in this line, let us indulge our vanity by saying that we yield to none other as a caterer to the *physical* man, whatever our shortcoming in regard to intellectual pabulum.) But as we have said, we feel that we have made a step in advance. It has been and still *is* our aim, to lay the foundation of a reliable newspaper, such as the rapidly increasing population, and the developing interests of our pet New Territory demand. So far as literary ability is concerned, we make no claims for the past. The public can readily judge how far we *could* devote ourselves to the nice details of "fine writing," un-

END OF THE FIRST VOLUME

MASTHEAD AND LEADER in the first anniversary edition of THE ENTERPRISE, when it was being published at Carson City.

By 1881, when W. L. Jernegan lay dying in White Pine, THE TERRI-
TORIAL ENTERPRISE had been for two full decades the newspaper terror,
wonder, and amazement of the Western nation. It had made fortunes for
its owners, had recorded at intimate firsthand some of the great moments
in the history of the continent and of the world. It had spawned celebrated
writers as no other American newspaper had ever done, with the possible
exception of Charles Dana's *New York Sun*. It had fulfilled its destiny
as one of the radiant and romantic properties of a golden age in history and
its immortality was secure so long as the memory of man should run.

"The nerve center of Washoe, the brainiest sheet on the Coast," Dr.
George D. Lyman was to call THE ENTERPRISE in the 'sixties. "It had acquired enormous prestige. It could make any man in the Territory. It was
honest and fearless. It might fear God—but no puny man. It was the
mouthpiece of Sun Mountain—her final tribunal—her judge and advocate.
It could be loved; it could be feared like the plague. When it got angry
it had claws like those of a mountain cat. It was Comstock to the core—the
mirror of her astounding personality."

This was what W. L. Jernegan had sold for a pitiful pittance, and it
was on this that W. L. Jernegan laid so swinging and incendiary a maledic-
tion that Jernegan's Curse has passed into the lexicon of the Old West and
become folklore.

Raising himself for the last time on his pillow, the old man wished
great and lasting evils upon THE TERRITORIAL ENTERPRISE and all those
who had heretofore, did now or might in future participate in its conduct
or fortunes. He cursed its plant and premises, mildewing with invective
its stock of paper in the storerooms, melting its type in their cases with his
accomplished blasphemy, loosing the presses on their bedplates and wish-
ing an eternal pi on every character in its fonts of agate, brevier, pearl,
diamond, Barnum, and Old Style. Widening his scope to be more in-
clusive, W. L. Jernegan rose to heights of oratory that would have bemused
great Webster. He invoked damnation and anathema on the Comstock
that had brought prosperity to THE ENTERPRISE, he conjured doom for the
entire State of Nevada, by counties and townships, by sections and quarter
sections. In a magnificent peroration, a mighty coda of superlatives to end
all execrations forever, like Sir Balaam in Pope's poem, he cursed God.

Tired but happy, W. L. Jernegan then departed this world.

Because of its character and individuality as territorial and shortly
state capital, Carson City established a well-defined tradition of journalism
all its own, and it is interesting, if not precisely profitable, to speculate on

18

what would have been its destiny had THE TERRITORIAL ENTERPRISE chosen to remain there rather than risk the hazards of its ascent to the Comstock.

Certainly it would not have achieved the heroic stature it assumed as the leading organ of news and opinion in the cosmopolis of the Western World. While its annals cannot be described as tranquil, Carson never participated in the free-wheeling razzle-dazzle of its rich and uninhibited neighbor. It never shared the florid overtones of hurrah which were the breath of life in Virginia City, nor did it participate in the impious journalistic gavottes to which editors of THE ENTERPRISE were inspired by the midst in which they operated.

But first and last, Carson's newspapers had their moments.

One of the most enchanting hoaxes in a generation when the press considered the hoax the highest form of humor was evolved by the editors of the *Carson Appeal* in the 'seventies. So venomous were the *Appeal*'s feuds with its contemporaries and so dangerous the wit and erudition of its staff that after a time rival editors refused to tangle with it on matters of state or civic policy. The *Appeal* was invariably victorious in controversy and none dared cross its path.

In desperation its editors looked about for someone to beat about the ears. Not a victim offered itself until a wholly imaginary adversary appeared in the form of the *Wabuska Mangler*. Wabuska, a country crossroads at sufficient remove from Carson City to discourage investigation, boasted a single general store, a saloon, and half a dozen dwellings. Later it was to be a water stop on the Carson & Colorado Railroad, but at no time in its history did it ever boast or even pretend to a newspaper. The *Mangler* existed in the imagining of the *Appeal* alone and a horrid threat indeed it represented to decent society.

The *Mangler*, the *Appeal* declared, was a disgrace to the newspaper profession, a blot on the scutcheon of Nevada's fair name, a hissing and byword among the godly. Its editors, scoundrels and blackguards to a man, deserved hanging. They ought to be ashamed of themselves and so well and unfavorably were they known that none ever dared show his face in virtuous and upstanding Carson City. The *Mangler* traded in subversion, it was reputedly implicated in a papist plot to overthrow the country by force; its works were as a troubled sea and salvation was far from it.

Whenever the *Appeal* needed a whipping boy the *Mangler* was paraded as a horrible example. But the hoax got out of hand. A now forgotten outrage in the *Mangler*'s columns incited to violence a group of civic-minded Carson Cityans. They organized a posse, purchased a quantity of rope, and announced that they, joined and augmented by any patriots and right-thinking folk who might be so minded, would next day go up against the citadel of Wabuska and lynch the depraved and thrice-damned editors of the *Mangler*.

The *Appeal* rushed into print, before the anabasis could be mounted, with the intelligence that the dastards who managed the affairs of the *Mangler* had caught wind of impending retribution. They had packed their plant and fled the state in hacks with drawn blinds and had sought refuge none knew where. Cool heads should now prevail, the *Appeal* suggested, to call off the expeditionary force.

The project was shelved, but so firmly established was its reputation for wickedness that years later, according to Wells Drury, Nevadans continued to cite the spectral *Wabuska Mangler* as an example of depravity, and occasional savage denunciations of its memory in the *Appeal* kept it odiously green.

Most notable of the Carson City school of newspaper editors was the brilliant but alarming Sam Davis, brother of the incomparable Bob, whose column of travels, "Bob Davis Recalls," for many years ornamented the *New York Sun* of fragrant memory.

Differing with Sam Davis was apt to be dangerous. Upon one occasion he encountered a hated rival, C. N. Harris, editor of the *Index*, in a corridor of the state capitol. Davis rushed upon him with Ojibway screeches of hate and defiance and dealt the fellow so stout a blow with his walking cane that Harris was rendered insensible.

Fined $75 in district court, Davis paid under protest and declared that he had broken a fine Malacca stick beyond all repairing and that the combined fine and value of his cane were more than the smiting had been worth.

In such an atmosphere of rugged individualism one may well speculate on the role THE TERRITORIAL ENTERPRISE would have played had it not joined the ever rising tide of fortune seekers who set their faces toward the ineffable promise of the Comstock.

Season In The Sun

IT SEEMS improbable that any bonanza in precious metals in the world's history has ever been exploited in such a bonanza of superlatives as those evoked to tell the Comstock story. So improbable were the details of life, love, larceny, litigation, and even legitimate enterprise in Virginia City during its productive years that for more than a quarter of a century the superlative somehow partook of understatement.

Paradox piled upon metaphor and simile upon statistic, millions of words of them, describing the riches and their consequences of Sun Mountain, and still left the story only half told.

It is a tenable thesis that one source and one alone could tell in its entirety the chronicle of the Comstock Lode in its years of teem: a complete file of THE TERRITORIAL ENTERPRISE.

It does not exist.

During the months of THE ENTERPRISE' Carson City interlude, brave doings had been toward in Virginia City. The first discoverers, Peter O'Riley and Pat McLaughlin, continued to work their rockers profitably while Old Pancake Comstock and Old Virginny Finney, by now joined in their muscle act by a Manny Penrod, superintended operations, talked grandly of the future, and did no lick of work that anybody was afterward able to recall. Prospectors with claims down the hill in Gold Canyon moved up to stake diggings near the profitable outcroppings and overflowed into an adjacent ravine known as Six Mile Canyon. According to the standards of the Comstock's first discoverers, everyone was getting rich, but in the light of later events their ores could only be described as "poor man's pudding."

The greatest single impediment, next to whisky and the sidewalk superintendents, encountered by O'Riley and McLaughlin was the thick blue clay which was uncovered in all the best pockets and outcroppings and which clogged their rockers and impeded everything. Mostly they discarded it when they could, searching specimens in free form or at worst in matrices more available to its recovery by the primitive processes at hand.

There were, however, inquiring minds in the diggings, and one fateful

21

day a curious pilgrim from Grass Valley over in the Sierra pocketed a specimen and took it home with him.

James Ott had set up an assay office in Grass Valley's Main Street back in 1853. He was a technician of respected authority in his field, and prospectors from the length and breadth of the Mother Lode sent specimens to his cupels, secure in the knowledge that his assays might be relied on. Through the teller's cage in Ott's office passed the specimen of Washoe blue clay. The assay was underwritten by Judge James Walsh, a leading citizen of Grass Valley.

James Ott was surprised at what turned up from his assay. So was Judge Walsh and, to eliminate any chance of error, Ott ran it again. It turned up better than $3,000 to the ton, not in the expected gold, but in silver.

The tremendous implications of the discovery were not lost on the man of law. Swearing Ott to secrecy, the judge confided his tidings to an old friend who providentially possessed a mule and prospecting outfit, Joe Woodworth, and sunrise found the pair making tracks out of Grass Valley with the intention of beating the world, which would obviously learn of this state of affairs before very long, to Virginia City.

As they achieved Donner Summit and paused to let the mule get his breath, Judge Walsh chanced to look backward over the trail they had just traversed. Then he swore a most unmagisterial oath and clutched Woodworth's sleeve. A mile or so behind was a large part of the population of Grass Valley, likewise urging mules to greater exertion and exhorting each other with cheery outcries in the direction of Nevada.

"That blabbermouth Ott," said the judge disgustedly. "We should have severed his carotid—cut his throat, that is—before leaving."

The exodus to Nevada that ensued became the classic gold rush of all time, depopulating the camps of the Mother Lode as they had originally drained off the population of San Francisco. So numerous were the participants in this latter-day anabasis into the Washoe hills that for weeks at a time no single vehicle westbound could breast the tide of men and animals headed eastward over the narrow roads in the High Sierra. The California mails halted at Carson and Genoa until the crest of immigration had passed. Men and mules, men on horseback, footmen packing their miner's tools on their backs and pushing them in barrows, small carts, stages, and in a few cases private carriages formed an irresistible torrent out of Hangtown, around the southern end of Lake Tahoe, and down the precipitous grades into Eagle Valley.

In Virginia City homeless thousands milled about in a riot of dusty inconvenience, hundreds living for months in holes bored into the mountain like gophers, others paying exorbitant prices to sleep in eight-hour shifts in shacks and tents crowded almost beyond human endurance. Law of any sort, drinking water, sanitary provisions, and civic organization were unknown. Veterans of previous gold rushes remarked that, compared to Virginia City, bedlam on Halloween was a study in pastoral tranquillity.

Names that were to make news in the almost immediate future abounded among the firstcomers.

Judge David S. Terry, a cloak-and-dagger ruffian who was already *persona ingratissima* in California, came to Washoe with a valise filled with Secessionist tracts. George Hearst, future United States Senator and future grandfather of a newspaper dynasty, was among the early arrivals.

William M. Stewart, sometime Yale man and shortly to be Nevada's patriarchal Senator and father of American mining law, heard the call. In far-off New Orleans a dusky beauty who called herself Julia Bulette and who was soon to fill columns of space in THE ENTERPRISE, read about the Comstock in the *Picayune* and took passage for Panama en route to the new golconda. One of Judge Walsh's neighbors back in Grass Valley got the news and the Rev. Patrick Manogue, a Jesuit and humanitarian, too, hiked up his cassock and hit for the silver diggings.

Adolph Sutro, Jewish cigar maker of San Francisco, one day to be mayor of that radiant city, came to Virginia City with engineering ideas which were not to be altogether popular. John Mackay, mining a poor man's claim at Downieville, and Jim Fair, destined between them to be princes of an empire of silver, hit the trail leading eastward. In their train followed Henry Yerington, whose bountiful whiskers were to be the hallmark of the swaggering Virginia & Truckee Railroad; Lucky Baldwin, who could do nothing wrong with money or right with women; Marcus Daly, a name that was to be blazoned over Montana in burnished copper; and gunmen, madames, gamblers, blacklegs, confidence men, drummers, bartenders from the Barbary Coast, hard rock miners from Amador, assayers, metallurgists, and shyster lawyers.

For *Harper's Monthly* came that crack correspondent and sketch artist, J. Ross Browne, who had covered the primal tumults of California and would still be filing dispatches at press rates when Geronimo was raising scalps outside of Tombstone.

And for THE TERRITORIAL ENTERPRISE there came footing it up through the Devil's Gate at Silver City—say the name with bugles—Joe Goodman,

23

PIONEER EDITOR OF THE COMSTOCK

JOE GOODMAN, Publisher of THE TERRITORIAL ENTERPRISE, as he
looked at the time of his arrival on the Comstock.

Joseph T. Goodman, Goodman of The Enterprise, first gentleman of the Comstock, discoverer of Mark Twain, poet, *beau sabreur*, a notable judge of Madeira, and first and last a newspaperman.

The word journalist had no place in Virginia City.

The entry upon the Comstock stage of its starred performers was strictly in accordance with the professional precedence and protocol of the time and place.

Pioneer among the merchants who foresaw in the crude diggings fortunes other than those implied by refractable ores was Charlie Sturm, who located Virginia City's first commercial venture, a bar comprising two boards suspended on barrels, at the southwest corner of A and Sutton streets, thereby establishing beyond all possibility of cavil the precise center of the town's business section to be. Well in advance of his time, Sturm installed the first plank floor the Comstock had seen and when, shortly thereafter, Wells Fargo's first Comstock agent, Dave Ward, set up his gold scales in a tent across the street, it was agreed that when Wells Fargo should erect a more permanent quarters Sturm should share it to the mutual satisfaction of all concerned. In a few months Wells Fargo did in fact build a frame office building and Sturm, his resort now appropriately known as "The Express Bar," moved into the basement.

On a third corner was the tent which housed the corporation offices of Penrod, Comstock & Co., primeval bonanza firm which was shortly to sell out for peanuts and disappear from the scene forever.

The fourth corner site at Sutton and A, the northwest one, was appropriated by The Territorial Enterprise. Thus the essentials of urban progress—express and banking, a stock brokerage, whisky slings, and its own newspaper—were all concentrated on the Comstock within handy conversational distance of one another if one only raised his voice a little above the shouting of the stage drivers in Sturm's place. It was a handy arrangement.

The importance of the Express Bar as an annex of business at A and Sutton, generally, but especially of The Enterprise, must not be underestimated. The first business premises in every frontier community in the West was, by immutable convention, a saloon. From Columbia to Downieville on the Mother Lode the earliest tent, shack, or lean-to of the diggings was a bar. The same thing obtained from Alder Gulch and Bannock in Montana Territory to Cherry Creek and Central City in Colorado. Doors that swung both ways were the first to be hung in the cow towns of Dodge City, Abilene, Newton, and Hays. The first length of wrought-iron pipe to see service in Julesburg, Cheyenne, Corinne, and Promontory was not a conduit for water but accommodation for the boots of the pioneers before the pine or mahogany artifact which proclaimed that civilization had arrived. The tradition obtained to the very end, when the last of all bonanzas was uncovered at Goldfield, Nevada, at the turn of the century. The first business structure to arrive in town was a saloon drawn across the desert on skids by ox team from neighboring Tonopah.

In his "Silver Kings," Oscar Lewis, perhaps the most conservative and reliable of all Comstock historians, comments at length on the capacity of Virginia City for strong waters. "For years [says Mr. Lewis] Washoe residents were known all over the Coast as accomplished tipplers; it was a well earned distinction. During the first two years the camps on both sides of the Divide had five saloons to every establishment dealing in other commodities. . . . In 1880, when the Lode was already on the down grade, the per capita consumption of Virginia City was twenty-two and a half gallons a year, one third of which was whisky; yet 1880 was called a dry year in comparison to 1876."

And it might be remarked that, compared to 1860, when the Comstock had no water supply at all and what was vended from door to door at five cents a glass was popularly supposed to contain strychnine, 1876 was a dry year, too.

The tradition of hard drinking has never entirely disappeared from Virginia City and as recently as 1953 THE TERRITORIAL ENTERPRISE proudly proclaimed, "Survey Shows Virginia City To Be Drinkingest Town in Entire U.S." This brag was based on a survey in *Fortune* magazine which demonstrated that, with an average of one saloon to each 207 inhabitants, the State of Nevada easily took the sweepstakes as America's wettest commonwealth. THE ENTERPRISE pointed out that Virginia City, with one saloon to every twenty inhabitants, topped the Nevada average and hence ranked the entire nation in alcoholic content. "Nevada," said *Fortune*, "is one great big twenty-four-hour-a-day barroom." "Virginia City is the drinkingest community in the United States and perhaps the universe," said THE ENTERPRISE.

THE ENTERPRISE moved to the Comstock just as the last of its original discoverers were being eased, or in some cases sluiced, down the side of Sun Mountain. Like the founders of the fortunes of Nevada's first newspaper, one and all, the primal pioneers sold out before their properties reached anything like profitable production. Old Pancake Comstock, who

EDITORIAL ROOMS, NEVADA STYLE

LITHOGRAPHS of the fine steam locomotive engines being outshopped by Matthias Baldwin at Philadelphia, costly crystal lighting fixtures, and an amazement of capacious spittoons, characterized the decor of the Old Magnolia Saloon in Virginia City, which remained open twenty-four hours a day for the convenience of THE ENTERPRISE owners and editorial staff. Printers and compositors favored the Philadelphia Brewery or the Boca Springs Saloon, the latter located at No. 7 South C Street, and convenient to THE ENTERPRISE either for a quick one or more extended communion with "the ardent."

sold for a trifling $11,000 the property he had larcenously acquired from O'Riley and McLaughlin, ended a few years later a suicide in Montana. Old Virginny Finney, who gave his name to the cosmopolis of the Western World, contrived to stay in a state of alcoholic exaltation on his winnings, until he fell from his horse and broke his neck. Alvah Gould, whose half share in the Gould & Curry Mine would in a few years have netted him a cool $8,000,000, sold out for $450 and ended his days symbolically enough running a peanut stand in Reno. O'Riley and McLaughlin, who together had held out for the biggest of all bonanzas to date, a miraculous $40,000, both died to be buried at public expense.

The age of the true inheritors of the Comstock's riches was at hand. So were the great days of THE TERRITORIAL ENTERPRISE.

On Saturday, November 3, 1860, the first weekly issue of THE ENTERPRISE to appear under the date line Virginia City was published from the A and Sutton Street offices, with the firm name Williams & Wollard at the masthead. On Saturday, March 23 of the following year, the historic names of Jonathan Williams, J. T. Goodman, and Dennis McCarthy appeared as owners, and soon thereafter, so great was the rise in its fortunes together with those of the Comstock itself, THE TERRITORIAL ENTERPRISE appeared as Nevada's first daily.

Soon, too, Williams withdrew from the partnership. Publication six times a week, he explained, "was a little too rapid for him." Dan De Quille afterward pictured him as a rough and ready sort of editorial chief who cared nothing for grammar or spelling and whose copy was "licked into shape," in the homely phrase of the day, by the compositors at their type cases.

"I get ideas and just slap them down as they come into my head," he told De Quille one evening over a glass of something stronger than water, at the International Bar. "As I hand it in my copy is pretty rough hewn but it comes out fine in the morning. Sometimes it surprises me." Perhaps Joe Goodman "hit it a lick on the way through the composing room," Williams suspected. He died of an overdose of laudanum a few years later.

Wollard, a man of mystery, appears to have been a Carson City restaurateur and friend of Williams, who advanced money for early financing of the paper and for bringing it up the grade to the Comstock. After the money was repaid he disappeared.

The story of THE ENTERPRISE in its early years is a story of perfect timing. Almost at the very moment that Goodman and McCarthy assumed complete ownership, it became established that the Comstock's surface diggings and ores of easily accessible outcroppings were actually the merest superficial traces of incalculable bonanzas which would be available to deep mining.

Ownership of mining claims was measured in feet held along the presumed face of the Lode, and owners of seemingly trivial footage in Gould & Curry, Hale & Norcross, Ophir, Best & Belcher, Kentuck, Burning Moscow, Crown Point, Yellow Jacket, and other Comstock properties were assured of millions as soon as methods of recovering and milling should be devised for the ore bodies which extended far below the surface of Sun Mountain. The classic example of the possibilities of footage casually acquired was that of Eilley Orrum, the camp's first laundress and boardinghouse keeper, who owned a few feet at the Gold Hill end of the Lode. The ten feet immediately adjacent was the property of a good-natured illiterate named Sandy Bowers, whom Eilley shortly married. Their combined twenty feet of the Comstock proved to embrace fantastically rich workings and Sandy and Eilley were Nevada's first silver millionaires.

The fortunes of any prudently managed newspaper property in such surroundings could hardly fail to prosper—and the management of Goodman and McCarthy was prudent.

Almost from its first beginnings in Virginia City, the affairs of THE ENTERPRISE assumed an accelerated tempo, and the paper itself was destined to become the pattern and archetype of all Western newspapers in pioneer times. Its gunfighting editors, celebrated news beats, authority and power in affairs of state, and its hilarious and uninhibited way of life were to become legendary, the glass of journalistic fashion which was to find its counterpart in every frontier paper from Alder Gulch to Durango and from Bodie to the Black Hills.

Newspapermen of the time commonly carried arms and had frequent recourse to them, so that the Colt's Navy .41, a favored weapon of the period, was as familiar a property to publication offices as type case and imposing stone.

His first day on duty as a reporter for the *Gold Hill News*, Wells Drury later recalled, the rest of the staff went to lunch leaving him in charge of the office. His first caller was a shady political colonel in a state of incandescent rage over some fancied editorial slight, who brandished a bullsnake whip and shouted for the editor's tripes. Drury had never before handled firearms but there was a large black revolver handy on his desk and pointing it in the direction of the complainant, he was gratified when.

it exploded with a terrific roar and a cloud of black powder smoke. The diminutive Drury, then a lad in his teens, pursued the fleeing politico through town, punctuating his screams for mercy with gunfire as the entire community turned out to cheer and applaud the spectacle.

A reporter on the neighboring *Eureka Sentinel* at about this time was shot and killed in the main street of Eureka, before he could draw his own weapon, by a first citizen who imagined his wife's name had been sullied in a news story.

In Bodie a pitched battle was staged between one of that tumultuous town's political factions and the staff of the *Bodie Free Press*, in which both sides sustained casualties; and over in the Cherry Creek Diggings in Colorado the offices of the newly founded *Rocky Mountain News* existed for several days in a state of siege by lawless elements, while editors and compositors alike manned Henry repeating rifles at the windows and copy boys and printer's devils ran the blockade for ammunition from the town's hardware stores. The *News'* founder, William N. Byers, was kidnaped by armed ruffians with the avowed intention of "stopping his attacks by stopping his breath," and rescued in the nick of time from lynching at the Criterion Saloon by a mounted posse of reporters and printers who charged the stronghold of lawlessness in cavalry formation. In a counterattack upon the *News* offices, George Steele, one of the most notorious gunmen of Denver's early days, was shot from the saddle, "the entire side of his head blown away and his brain freely exposed." Byers was credited with the lethal marksmanship.

The advice of a veteran reporter to a new recruit on a frontier newspaper was "never to split an infinitive and be sure all his nipples were capped," the latter a reference to the arming of the cap and ball revolvers of the time.

Bohemian was the word for THE ENTERPRISE in its first days on the Comstock. The staff bunked in a decrepit lean-to attached to the side of the editorial and printing offices. The roof was so leaky in winter that leaders of string festooned the ceiling to divert the flow of melting snow from type cases and other machinery. Three meals a day were served by Old Joe the Chinese cook and for a time were eaten off the imposing stone for lack of other table.

The printer's devil, a wicked young man named Noyes who was constantly hungry, maintained a running feud with Old Joe by stealing from his pantry, and the process of putting the paper to bed on printing day was often interrupted by a mad chase staged by Joe and the devil through

ATMOSPHERE of the A and Sutton Street premises of THE ENTERPRISE is reproduced in the drawing above by the distinguished Western artist E. S. Hammack. On the stairway is Dennis McCarthy; leaning against his type cases is Steve Gillis and behind the Washington hand press is Noyes, the always hungry printer's devil. On the imposing stone in the foreground is the Colt's Navy revolver of frontier convention. Of the paper at this time Joe Goodman wrote: "THE ENTERPRISE is published at three times the cost of any other paper in the state . . . In order to regul this we are compelled to charge higher prices for advertising space." J. Ross Browne drew the sketch at right, but editors of THE ENTERPRISE were instructed to resist such intimidation whenever possible.

the composing room and into the street outside. Sobriety was not a distinguishing characteristic of the staff and tall ones were rushed in a continuous Niagara from Sturm's Saloon across the way.

At first the paper's finances were of an insecure nature, and the payment in advance of a new subscription or for an advertising insertion was celebrated with a fine steak dinner, while for the next several days the table fare might be of a far more modest order.

But, in common with the fantastic boom times in the region it served, THE ENTERPRISE soon came upon blue days and fair. The roof was patched. Steak appeared on the menu every day. Handsome new type was ordered to replace the worn brevier and agate that had seen service on the *Sacramento Union*. Both the owners had new frock coats of best English broadcloth, and Goodman, an amateur of fine wines, drank vintage claret every night at the restaurant of the International Hotel. Times were good.

"Mr. Goodman and another journeyman printer had borrowed forty dollars," wrote an admiring contemporary, "and set out to try their fortune in the city of Virginia. They found THE TERRITORIAL ENTERPRISE a poverty-stricken weekly, gasping for breath and likely to die. The editors and printers slept on the floor, a Chinaman did the cooking and the imposing stone was the general dinner table . . . But things have changed. The paper is a great daily printed by steam. There are five editors and twenty-three compositors and the subscription price is $16 a year, the advertising rate exorbitant and the columns crowded. The paper is clearing from six to ten thousand dollars a month."

Virginia City legend has it that Goodman and McCarthy every Saturday night divided the take in equal halves and each one carried his share home in a fire bucket filled with gold double eagles.

The stay of THE ENTERPRISE at its first Virginia City address at the corner of A and Sutton streets was brief. Within two years it was apparent that the business center of town was gravitating downhill toward the east and that C Street was destined to be the main thoroughfare and artery of commerce. THE ENTERPRISE once more unbolted its press from its bedplates, packed its type cases, and prepared to move. It relocated in the upper floor of a two-story wooden frame structure in North C Street on a site later occupied by Molinelli's Hotel. Downstairs was Joe Barnert's clothing store and next door was an old neighbor, Wells Fargo, who had also heeded the times and come downtown.

The life and times of THE TERRITORIAL ENTERPRISE in Virginia City's crescent years were characterized by an atmosphere of unabashed hooray.

The pretensions to holy endeavor and elevated moral tone which came to American journalism in a later time and which are possessed of all the plausibility of an opera hat on a Pawnee were unknown to an earlier generation of practitioners. Editors made no claims as guardians of public morals and seldom boasted of their wakeful vigilance of heart as preceptors of universal virtue. The right-thinking, forward-looking, and professional ethics to which modern newspaper publishers lay claim would have reduced Joe Goodman or Dennis McCarthy to inextinguishable laughter.

American journalism was then as it has always been, a hilarious and disreputable calling which fetched the fancy of uninhibited practitioners of chicane and fraudulence. But it never, as is the fashion of a fraudulent age, assumed the mantle of prophetic dignity which was imagined by the Pulitzers, Reids, and Ochses of a later generation. No schools of journalism existed to elevate the spurious to the exalted level of fictitious respectability.

A case in point may be cited to include Dennis McCarthy, Goodman's associate, at a later date, when McCarthy had quit THE ENTERPRISE and was editing the *Virginia Chronicle*. Under McCarthy's direction, the Comstock's wealthy Virginia & Truckee Railroad, owned and operated by the satraps of the Bank of California, was subjected to ferocious editorial heckling and abuse. At the period in question the *Chronicle* was little more than a blackmailing operation and its conduct was dictated, not by any selfless dedication to the general weal so much as in the hope that the railroad's owners would tire of its nuisance value and buy it out at an exorbitant figure. McCarthy's asking price was a fantastic $50,000. When a few years later the *Chronicle* did indeed close up shop, it was sold for less than $500.

Henry Yerington, Darius Ogden Mills' viceroy in Carson City, was instructed to abate McCarthy's rage and offered the editor a flat $150 monthly to call off the dogs. Already—this was the late 'seventies—pretensions to professional respectability were beginning to undermine the once honest rascality of the calling and McCarthy spurned the bribe. He did, however, settle for the precise equivalent in advertising for the *Chronicle* and free passes for himself and his staff and family over the railroad. Yerington was able to write to Mills: "McCarthy has come to terms for $150 advertising per month and the passes and agrees to wheel into line, quit his abuse of you and act like a white man from now on."

Joe Goodman, the genius of THE ENTERPRISE, in whose ownership the paper became "the mirror of Washoe's audacious life—the vade mecum of every mining town," was described by George Lyman as "handsome, reckless, daredevil, a youth of parts," every product of whose pen was marked by quality and good taste and who, to an entire generation, was the prototype of the old-time frontier editor.

Before the Washoe excitements got into his blood, Goodman had been one of San Francisco's gilded age of Bohemians and a staff member of the *Golden Era* in the years when that swashbuckling feuilleton had been the favorite publication for the insertion of challenges to duels between editors, legislators, and other public figures of Montgomery Street. A perfectionist in many fields of knowledge ranging from vintage Bordeaux to the epigrams of Catullus and odes of Horace, he was an expert printer who could compose at the type cases without written copy an editorial to rock senators on their congress gaiters or graceful occasional verses, as the moment might require.

A drinking companion who was still singing "John Peel" when other participants in symposiums at Barnum's Restaurant in C Street were under the table, Goodman had no pretensions to imaginary professional ethics, but insisted on getting out a readable newspaper in first-class style.

On one occasion, which was remembered by old-time type slingers on the Comstock with horror for decades to come, a careless compositor and his assistant contrived to drop the forms containing the entire center spread of THE ENTERPRISE onto the composing-room floor in a pi of catastrophic proportions. The paper, in order to meet its press time, appeared with its two center pages a blank and the rival *Gold Hill News* reported that the town alcoholic had clutched at his eyes and collapsed on the bar screaming that he was blind; THE ENTERPRISE was a blank in front of his face! Goodman laughed heartily with the rest of Virginia City and discharged the guilty printers instanter and without appeal.

Goodman's familiarity with the classical humanities in no way exempted him from the less elevated frontier repartee of the time and place.

Of an inquiring and conversational mind, one day in the bar of the Sazarac he observed a patron reading a copy of the *Daily Old Piute* with which THE ENTERPRISE was at the moment on chilly terms. "Tell me, friend," Goodman asked civilly. "What do you find to read that's instructive in that paper?"

"Oh," retorted the heretic, recognizing the publisher of THE ENTERPRISE, "I read the *Piute* to get the news. I use THE ENTERPRISE to wipe my behind with."

"Keep right on as you are, friend," said Goodman evenly, "and in a short time your behind will know more than your head ever will."

Well in advance of what was later to become celebrated as sensational metropolitan journalism, THE ENTERPRISE filled its columns from the beginning with shootings and stabbings, infidelities, suicides, assaults, embezzlements, and excursions into lawlessness. A new reporter on his first day as a member of the staff went on his initial assignment to the Divide which separated Gold Hill from Virginia City, only to find his first report to the paper was to describe the murder of a close friend. Violence in the saloons of C Street was so commonplace and musicians in such oversupply that when a giant miner in Jacob Wimmer's Virginia Hotel was about to toss an adversary over his head and through a window, somebody shouted: "Don't waste him! Kill a fiddler with him!" Suicides by poison were so frequent among the prostitutes on The Line that such occasions rarely warranted more than a single line of type in an obscure part of the paper. When a customer in one of the town's billiard saloons was stabbed to death one evening during a friendly game of pool, Sam Davis, one of the foremost contemporary historians, recounted that his body lay where it fell half under the table until noontime the next day. The coroner was unable to arrive before that time to authorize its removal, and participants in the game were at some inconvenience to straddle the dead man in order to make their shots.

Unhappily for the practical-minded student of such matters, the details of THE ENTERPRISE manufacture and its business economy are not available to posterity. Its circulation, advertising rates, the number of its compositors and printers, even the specific types of machinery which entered into its production—all the records which may have been kept of the details of its conduct as a business were lost in the Great Fire of 1875.

In its declining years, when its circulation was probably greater and its prestige much less, Joe Farnsworth, later State Printer at Carson City but then a delivery boy, remembers that the press run was never in excess of 1,500 copies. In the 'sixties, when the population of the Comstock ranged between 10,000 and 15,000 and newsprint was far more durable, so that a single paper might be passed from hand to hand by a score of readers, it is doubtful its circulation rose much above that figure. Until the coming of its first steam press in 1864, THE ENTERPRISE' mechanical limitations would have made any greater press run out of the question.

In the matter of finances, Wells Drury reprints the current estimate that Goodman and McCarthy netted between them better than $1,000 in gold

a day, a figure which at this remove and in the light of the then purchasing power of the hard dollar, seems astronomically unlikely. The newspaper was a gold mine; it undeniably shared in the generally inflated fortunes of a fantastic mining boom, but $1,000 daily profit would seem an optimistic estimate.

And there was, of course, competition both for the circulation and for the advertising revenue of Goodman's paper.

Although it was to outlast all its early contemporaries and achieve a wider celebrity than any of them, THE TERRITORIAL ENTERPRISE' first years in Virginia City saw it in the company of a bewildering multiplicity of other newspapers. More than one paper in frontier communities was fairly commonplace. Bodie, in its great days, had three; Carson, first and last, half a dozen, but the Comstock saw the emergence and subsequent decline of so many journals of opinion, some of them after only the briefest life span, that their record is probably incomplete.

Among the earliest were the *Trespass*, the *Daily Safeguard, Virginia Evening Bulletin, Daily Democratic Standard*, and the *Occidental*, the last of which was edited for a time by the prolific and ubiquitous Tom Fitch. There was also the *Daily Old Piute*, the *Nevada Pioneer*, a German-language semiweekly, and another German paper, the *Nevada Staats Zeitung*. The year 1864, which was characterized by a contemporary as "a sort of Fourth of July year for newspapers in Nevada," saw the brief flowering of the *Washoe Daily Evening Herald*, in whose publication Fitch was also associated for three short weeks with H. C. Bennett in an effort to arouse enthusiasm for Republican principles. The next year there appeared the equally Republican *Two O'Clock News*, still another German-language paper, the *Deutsche Union*, and the *Virginia Evening Chronicle*, which was to survive until comparatively recent times and with which, after its suspension as an independent property in 1916, THE TERRITORIAL ENTERPRISE was to be merged.

And to this already ample roster of Comstock publications during the early 'sixties there must be added the *Virginia Daily Union*, of which, once more, Fitch was the leading editorial spirit, and which was destined to tangle with THE ENTERPRISE in the most celebrated shooting in the Virginia City record.

Like the *Sacramento Union*, which from the very beginnings of the West's great days had made a special feature of its mining camp coverage and boasted that wherever pay ore showed in an assay, a *Union* correspondent or stringer would be on the scene within a week, THE ENTER-

PRISE made a good thing of news from the California-Nevada bonanzas and near bonanzas. It maintained part-time correspondents everywhere— Sam Clemens represented it in Aurora before coming to the home office—and its reporters interviewed every dusty prospector emerging from the desert solitudes and every stage driver who might be a repository of mining news or rumor from beyond the horizon.

News of the great world was received in the form of letter correspondence from Horace Greeley's venerated *New York Tribune* and for a time, until the completion of the Overland Telegraph obviated its usefulness, news letters were received by Pony Express from St. Joseph. Wells Fargo and THE ENTERPRISE shared the cost of maintaining a connecting pony on the banks of Carson River at the foot of Gold Canyon, to hurry up the hill with dispatches thrown off without stopping by the Pony Express rider on the run between Fort Churchill and Carson City. When the news was of great urgency, such as the firing on Fort Sumter, special bulletins were posted outside THE ENTERPRISE offices to tell in brief what would later be detailed in the early editions.

Even after almost a century the advertising columns of THE ENTERPRISE by the mid-'sixties seem crowded in a manner to light the eye of any business office executive today. Display insertions of more than a column's width were unknown, but seven two-inch columns to a page carried thousands of daily lines agate of the most profitable sort of business.

No lock-picker or thimble-rigger was required, so deposed the Messrs. Tilton & McFarland, safemakers of San Francisco, to operate the Lillie lock fabricated by a rival manufacturer. A single blow of a hammer against the safe door was sufficient to break the cast iron bolt of a Lillie lock and admit improperly accredited parties to the inner vault. But Tilton & McFarland's own safes were impervious to the most skilled yeggs and bank robbers and a fine assortment of these strong boxes could be seen at 318 Battery Street.

Advertising technique of the 'sixties was not above discrediting a rival product, no sir!

The Pioneer Stage Company's Concords went through daily between San Francisco and Virginia in twenty-four hours, "crossing the mountains by daylight." "Ho! For the Humboldt!" cried the Overland Mail Company, "Via Six Horse Stages! Tri-Weekly for Unionville and Star City via Ragtown and Stillwater." They carried the United States Mail and the pressing business of Wells Fargo & Co.

Gillig, Mott & Co., occupying the fireproof building at C and Taylor streets, offered at the lowest prices 25,000 pounds of boiler plate, 48,000 feet of gas pipe, 20,000 carriage bolts all sizes, 1,000 kegs of blasting powder, 400 metal wheelbarrows, and 600 globe valves (whatever they were).

It was wartime, and twenty men were wanted to "rally round the flag" in Captain Warner's Company of Nevada volunteers.

It was time for new type for THE TERRITORIAL ENTERPRISE, and James Connor's Sons Type Foundry, "Everything for the News or Job Office," were proud to say they had supplied it.

And the saloons of Virginia City, then and now the drinkingest community in all the wide, wonderful, boozy world—what profligate enchantments were not latent in the mere roll call of their names, perfumed with intimate association and Old Noble Treble Crown Whisky!

There was Jacob Wimmer's Virginia Hotel, which carried in its name a double significance since it was a hotbed of Secessionist sympathies; there was Tom Peasley's Sazarac, named for a new and important cocktail reportedly brought to Nevada from New Orleans by Julia Bulette, the camp's first and most gorgeous courtesan; there was the International Hotel, one of three structures to succeed one another by that fragrant name; and there was Barnum's Restaurant, where the nabobs of Chollar-Potosi and Hale & Norcross forgathered nightly. There was Chauvel's French Restaurant with a menu delectable with antelope steaks and the latest entrees from Delmonico's; there was The Roadside Club, favored of sporting gentry; the Café de Paris; El Dorado gaming rooms, where drinks were plentiful and generous as a matter of course; there were Pat Lynch's Place, The Old Magnolia, The Smokery, Gentry & Crittenden's, and The Howling Wilderness, a premises which never at any hour of the twenty-four betrayed the promise of commotional doings implicit in its name. There were more than one hundred saloons to choose from.

Nobody needed be sober for so much as a single moment in Virginia City. It was a splendid newspaper town.

Swords and Four Roses

N KEEPING with the age which saw it flourish, THE ENTERPRISE loved a fight. Elsewhere on the Comstock, feuds raged unabated and their participants resorted to eye gouging and chewing off the ears of the opposition or to the code duello, as their social status or pretensions to it inclined them. In the courts of law it is a notable circumstance that the first of the Comstock's banner crop of millionaire men was neither a prospector nor a mine owner and investor in mining properties, but William Morris Stewart, the bearded barrister from Yale whose services in mining litigation won him fees running to $100,000 and the title of "Father of American Mining Law."

Smiting the Amalekites hip and thigh beyond the walls of Kadesh was standard practice in the editorial rooms of THE ENTERPRISE. It smote almost anyone its whim indicated and not all its smiting was in the interest of high-minded endeavor, constructive civic thinking, or virtuous benevolence, nor was it governed by the wakeful vigilance of altruism so often associated with crusading newspapers, to hear their hired biographers tell it.

Sometimes editors and reporters of the paper took refuge in imagined alliances with lofty principles, but much of the time THE ENTERPRISE inclined to give the gardaloo or raspberry to the great and saintly just for the pure, uninhibited hell of it, and its spitballs were usually found to have been rolled in prussic acid.

Of the feuds in the record whose conclusion saw the enemies of THE ENTERPRISE lying in the gutters and spitting teeth, a few slender garlands culled from the deadly nightshade gardens of Sun Mountain will suffice.

In the early years of the editorship of Joe Goodman one of the most insistent rival editors was Tom Fitch of the *Virginia City Union*.* Fitch

* Tom Fitch, whose personal address and period-design oratory charmed both the Comstock and San Francisco for nearly two decades (among other celebrated speeches he made the address of the evening at the first of the great dinners at the Palace in honor of Phil Sheridan), is not to be confused with George Fitch, also a celebrated California editor of the time. George Fitch, at one time a proprietor of the *California Alta*, was also a figure of controversy. On one occasion he engaged in a notable exchange of fisticuffs with a detractor in the corridor of the Capitol at Sacramento, thus setting a precedent for more lethal encounter by his later namesake.

was a silver-tongued orator, a student of the classics, and possessed of a ready wit which delighted the Comstock for the better part of a generation.

At the funeral of William Ralston, the San Francisco Lorenzo whose death by drowning precipitated one of the worst of the Coast's many financial crises, Fitch pronounced the eulogy in the grand manner. "Commerce commemorated his deeds with her whitening sails and her laden wharves. There are churches whose heaven-kissing spires chronicle his donations. . . . He was the supporter of art; science leaned on him while her vision swept infinity. The footsteps of progress have been sandaled with his silver. He was the lifeblood of enterprise; he was the vigor of all progress; he was the epitome and representative of all that was broadening and uplifting in the life of California."

When delegates at a Republican convention who had been pledged to Fitch's candidacy for senatorial office bolted to another candidate, Fitch remarked bitterly: "I know how Lazarus felt; I too have been licked by dogs."

Trouble had been brewing between Fitch and THE ENTERPRISE at a low or domestic level for some time. The Fitch family had rooms in a boarding house which also was patronized by Dan De Quille and Mark Twain. Mrs. Anna Fitch, a kindhearted woman and celebrated for her pies, cakes, Cousin Jack pasties, and other kitchen products, often gave the boys the substance of a hearty midnight snack. Neither gratitude nor manners were any part of Twain's character at this stage in the game and he circulated a horrid rumor that he and Dan had hanged Mrs. Fitch's pet kitten, although it later appeared that the animal had merely strayed from home. They also robbed the Fitch woodbox, the then price of cordwood considered, an offense tantamount to horse stealing.

As the Constitutional Convention of 1863 loomed on the political horizon, Fitch bolted the Union party. His apostasy nearly cost him his life. THE ENTERPRISE had at the luckless politico with tar buckets and banshee screams. William Stewart, a staunch Unionist, set about kindling editorial bonfires in Goodman's paper that singed Fitch's coattails and set him leaping about C Street in sarabands of anguish. In the columns of the *Union*, Fitch remarked that the editorial policies of THE TERRITORIAL ENTERPRISE were suggestive of the love of God. Goodman was able to complete the tag to the effect that it "passeth all human understanding" and began shouting for his pistols.

Resort to the code duello, although sternly interdicted by law, was standard practice among editors and politicians both in California and

41

Nevada at the time. The assassination in San Francisco of James King of William by James Casey and the celebrated duel between David C. Broderick and Judge David S. Terry were still fresh in the general memory, but Virginia City had seen several killings on the field of honor and Nevada's last formal duel was not to be fought until 1876. The throwback to standards of romantic chivalry is generally attributed by historians to the strong Southern influence both in San Francisco and on the Comstock at the time. Silver-mounted pistols with set triggers were a property that appealed to the shady political colonels of mint julep and Cape jessamine persuasions.

At sunup on the morning of September 27, 1863, Joe Goodman and Tom Fitch were each driven in the company of their seconds and attending surgeons in shuttered hacks from Light & Allman's Livery Stable to Ingraham's Ranch in Stampede Valley. Goodman's fire-eating friend Major George Farrand, who had fought at Goliad and been with Sam Houston on the plains of San Jacinto, served for the publisher of THE ENTERPRISE. A Captain Roe and a Captain Fleeson, first names now unknown, seconded Fitch.

The weapons were Sam Colt's dragoon revolvers. This Colt was one of the deadliest hand guns of the frontier, weighing four pounds and firing a .44 caliber slug that could fell a running buffalo.

Virginia City's sporting element was present to a man: gamblers, pimps, touts, bartenders, teamsters, newspaper reporters, con men, shills, spielers, gold-brick artists, and snake-oil vendors. So many horse rigs and mounts had been rented in Virginia City that it was said there wasn't a saddle horse available in town. The odds were in favor of Goodman, who was known to have been coached by Major Farrand and who possessed a reputation for serenity of nerves not shared by the flighty and oratorical Fitch.

The long money won. At the appropriate count the adversaries turned and faced each other over thirty paces of Nevada desert. There was a single explosion as Goodman's revolver flashed and banged and Fitch sagged and fell on his face.

Whether guided by magnanimity or chance, Goodman's slug had torn away Fitch's kneecap and the editor walked with a pronounced limp for the rest of his life.

Not all the battles in which THE ENTERPRISE found itself involved had such lethal implications. Take the affair of "The Menken," for example.

Drama reporting on the Comstock had achieved a degree of critical sophistication in the 'sixties which was not to characterize its practice and

BLACK POWDER INTERLUDE

JOE GOODMAN'S duel with Tom Fitch of the *Union* was part of the pattern of the times in Nevada and California, where resort to the code duello was standard practice among newspapermen and politicians. Fatalities on the field of honor were by no means rare. Prevalence of dueling was laid to the strong influence of the Deep South, whose sons, bound for the West, brought ideals of chivalry along with the collected poems of Sidney Lanier, and recipes for mint juleps.

technique elsewhere for more than a decade to come. Virginia City in the golden noontide of "the road" was, with the single exception of San Francisco, the best theater town anywhere west of Chicago. Stock companies with name players of New York dimensions commonly made a practice of playing three nights or a week on the way to and from California, at Maguire's or Piper's Opera, and upon one notable occasion no fewer than five companies were playing in Shakespearean repertory in Virginia City on the same evening.

Helena Modjeska, Lotta Crabtree, Lola Montez, Edwin Booth, Salvini the Younger, Joseph Jefferson, and John McCullough regularly played to standing room only, with evening-dressed audiences who showered their favorites with gold double eagles as they took curtain calls in a manner at once gratifying and perilous to life and limb. One aged mumper who had been stunned by a gold slug which caught him in the temple as he bowed low over the footlights, regained his senses as fellow troupers filled his cupped hands with hard money that was his share of the windfall. "Ah, blessed wound!" he exclaimed.

And most of all, troupers admired to play Virginia City because good notices in THE TERRITORIAL ENTERPRISE carried all the prestige and importance of critical acclaim from William Winter in far-off New York. Drama critics on THE ENTERPRISE staff were hard to please and fair words in its columns were praise from Sir Hubert.

At the period of which we write THE ENTERPRISE arrived at its critical decisions in matters theatrical in a manner at once characteristic and unconventional. Three members of the staff, Joe Goodman, Dan De Quille, and Mark Twain, occasionally augmented by Joe Gillis, occupied aisle seats on opening nights. At the conclusion of the performance the friends met over a bottle of Mumm's or Moet in the bar of the International Hotel or one of John Piper's several handy taverns and pooled their reactions to the evening's entertainment. Having each contributed to this symposium, they chose one of their number either by lot or common consent to go to THE ENTERPRISE offices in South C Street and write next morning's review. The finished article embodied the joint critical opinions of four first-rate professionals and the streamlined editorial production of a single reporter.

Schism and dissension came to town with the advent on the Comstock of Adah Isaacs Menken in "Mazeppa," a spectacular melodrama reaching its climax in what today would be known as a production number, in which The Menken was borne offstage bound to the back of a coal-black

44

stallion to her presumable death in a dizzying mountain abyss. Mining towns throughout the West greeted "Mazeppa" and its star performer with hysterical enthusiasm. Crowds gathered at the Virginia & Truckee freight depot when the costarring stallion arrived via special handling in charge of Wells Fargo's express department. The Menken herself was serenaded by a firemen's choral society under her window in the International Hotel. The band from the American Engine Company No. 2 drowned out the singers. Miss Menken got a very handsome reception from Virginia City.

Maguire gave all his theatrical printing, posters, billboard work and such to THE ENTERPRISE job press, and on the opening night of "Mazeppa" the entire front row was segregated with red ribbons and a card reading "Reserved for the Staff of THE TERRITORIAL ENTERPRISE."

Trouble commenced when Joe, Dan, and Mark forgathered at the International after the final curtain in critical conference. Each was so convinced that his superlatives alone could do justice to the genius of The Menken that they could not decide who was to write the review. The Judgment of Paris was no more fraught with peril.

In the end there were three reviews printed in next morning's paper, each by a different drama critic but all unanimous in their raptures over "Mazeppa."

The Menken, reading THE ENTERPRISE in her suite at the International, was enchanted. Not so the rest of the company, no one of whom had received so much as mention in any of the three notices. At that evening's performance the supporting cast got thoroughly out of hand. There were ad libbed and uncomplimentary asides devoted to THE ENTERPRISE, none of them lost upon the audience. Bit players upstaged the star. Hitherto reliable troupers blew their lines. The stage became a shambles. The Menken retired to her dressing room in a towering rage and promptly canceled the rest of the engagement. Later, as cooler judgment prevailed, she relented and the show played out its promised week, but there was bad blood between Maguire and THE ENTERPRISE. The impresario withdrew his professional printing and gave it to the *Virginia Evening Bulletin*. THE ENTERPRISE block of free tickets for opening night was revoked. ENTERPRISE reporters were forbidden the premises on pain of summary ejection.

No man to take such indignities lying down, Joe Goodman ordered that the paper should carry no mention of Maguire or his productions except in unsavory context. Only the worst shows were reviewed by reporters, who had not, of course, been present and who drew liberally on their imaginations for unfavorable detail. Maguire was unable to book first-rate attractions or stars of consequence. Everyone was terrified of the terrible-tempered TERRITORIAL ENTERPRISE. Its savage accounts of companies with the temerity to play for Maguire were reprinted everywhere and, formerly the most sought-after theatrical town in the West, Virginia City was avoided by the profession as a plague spot.

In the end, faced by economic ruin, Maguire capitulated. THE ENTERPRISE' block of first night seats was again made available. Iced buckets of the best champagne appeared at their elbow when the three musketeers appeared for openings. Ushers lighted their cigars and assistant managers bowed deferentially. The printing contract was taken away from the *Bulletin* and returned to THE ENTERPRISE job press. Neither Maguire nor his successor as the Comstock's ranking impresario, John Piper, ever again undertook to buck the authority of THE ENTERPRISE. It didn't pay.

It might be remarked parenthetically that Maguire did not profit in wisdom from his losing skirmish with the Fourth Estate on the Comstock, but went on to bigger and more disastrous Waterloos in San Francisco, where he attempted to tangle with expert journalistic hatchet men in the persons of Charles and Mike de Young, youthful proprietors of the *Daily Dramatic Chronicle*. The matter was, of course, one of advertising, and when Maguire, in a moment of what can only be described as mistaken judgment, refused the *Chronicle* his business the de Youngs went at him with banshee screeches while calling for the tar buckets and hempen rope. "Maguire's life was one of those open books, interestingly read," said John Bruce in his story of San Francisco newspapers, *Gaudy Century*, "and the *Chronicle* disclosed that Maguire was not a person to be held up as an example to the young." Maguire ended in the gutter with his plug hat busted and spitting teeth while the de Youngs dusted their hands and went on to more magnificent blackmail.

Until more than forty years later, when the massed Shuberts attempted to do battle with the *New York Tribune*, Thespis took no such spectacular beating about the noggin.

Although the Pacific Railroad had been completed in 1869 and the frontier opened to adventurers aboard George Mortimer Pullman's Palace Cars, the West was possessed of an invincible fascination long after the buffalo were gone and hydraulic elevators were in operation in the hotels of San Francisco.

No amount of detailed chronicle, either fact or fiction, could surfeit the appetite for news of the West among readers in Boston's Beacon Street or gentlemen's clubs on Murray Hill. Profane periodicals such as *The*

NEVER A DULL MOMENT AT
THE ENTERPRISE

DURING the great bad feeling between
THE ENTERPRISE and John Piper (*at right*)
the paper made a practice of abusing all
performers booked by the unhappy impresario. Mostly the disgruntled mumpers
shook the dust of the Comstock from their
buskins, resolved never again to risk Nevada, but Irish-born Matilda Heron was not
one to take lying down a hostile notice of
her performance as Camille. "A wild, im-
pulsive, eccentric being," as she was later
described by William Winter, "and an ex-
ponent of the elemental passions," she appeared next morning demanding an inter-
view with the managing editor on duty.
The m.e. beat a fast retreat to The Old Magnolia, where no woman might follow, but
it was a close shave.

National Police Gazette and *The Illustrated Police News & Law Courts Recorder* regularly portrayed Last Chance Gulch and Bodie in terms of six-gun tumults, horsewhippings, and vigilante committees. More conservative publications like *Harper's Weekly* maintained accredited Western correspondents such as Rufus Zogbaum, Charles Graham, and J. Ross Browne, who sketched and reported the disappearing frontier with restraint and a high degree of literacy.

The *Life* magazine of the 1870's was *Frank Leslie's Illustrated Weekly Newspaper*, a blend of gee-whiz sensationalism and expert pictorial reporting, whose staff artists working the West for picture material included the team of Harry Ogden and Walter Yaeger and other uncommonly competent sketch artists and lithographers.

Even as late as 1877 the great American preoccupation with cowboys and Indians, plainsmen, scouts, and bonanzas was still in fullest stride, and Frank Leslie set about organizing a reportorial safari through the West that should bring to his readers the entire panorama of continental conquest and achievement in illustrated instalments of a comprehensive magnitude never yet undertaken.

To this end, a special Wagner Palace Sleeping Car was built to Leslie's specifications, including editorial rooms, luxurious living quarters, and a dark room for the use of staff photographers who were included in the group of "literary ladies and gentlemen" of the party. At Grand Central Depot the staff, accompanied by Mr. and Mrs. Leslie themselves and "a number of champagne baskets and significant looking hampers" departed amidst silk-hatted huzzas for what was to be far and away the most comfortably upholstered voyage of exploration of all time.

Inevitably the Frank Leslie Expedition arrived on the Comstock. The mines at the time were in their fullest and most opulent production. Daily accounts of their recurrent bonanzas were carried under the Virginia City date line to newspapers throughout the entire world. Reigning monarchs, presidents, nabobs, and great names arrived in almost hourly succession aboard their private cars on the Virginia & Truckee Railroad to see at firsthand the greatest single source of material wealth in history.

Frank Leslie, a man of inquiring mind and a shrewd judge of news values, was fascinated with the deep mines under Sun Mountain, their operations, technique, and personnel. Day after day his staff artists worked, depicting the great hoisting works of Best & Belcher, the fabulous Cornish pumps in Crown Point, the stamp mills which for miles lined Carson Water, making the night hideous and Nevada's millionaire men ever richer. And week after week *Leslie's* printed their sketches for the paper's ever crescent circulation.

Virginia City, used as it was to all kinds of polite attention, was well disposed toward Frank Leslie.

But not for long. As usual, it was the woman who broke up the honeymoon.

Mrs. Leslie wrote a book about her trip as a member of the expedition, and what she had to say about Virginia City, where her husband had established such amicable relations, shortly was curling the hair of readers in C Street and provoking THE ENTERPRISE to anguished demands for rope and vigilantes.

The Comstock, wrote Mrs. Leslie, was "dreary, desolate, homeless, uncomfortable, wicked and Godforsaken." Its inhabitants enjoyed no home life but pursued a shiftless existence in saloons and pool halls at deplorable remove from the elevating influences of domestic hearth and fireside. Without mincing words, the lady journalist spoke her mind that virtuous women were few and far between in the Cosmopolis of the Washoes and that the female population of Virginia City was almost wholly composed of abandoned hussies far gone in infamy and depraved conduct. "The population of Virginia City," she said in loud emphatic tones, "is largely masculine, very few women except of the worst class, and as few children."

Aside from their signal lack of ordinary prudence in reporting, Mrs. Leslie's sentiments were in the worst imaginable taste, not only for their divergence from fact in favor of sensational falsehood, but because she and her husband, and indeed all members of the Leslie party, had been received with genuine hospitality in Nevada and accorded every sort of municipal honor. Fifteen years earlier her observations might well have been justified, in the era when Julia Bulette and her girls were practically the entire female population; but in 1877 Virginia City was a community of homes and the refinements of life, recently acquired, to be sure, and therefore doubly cherished and invested with sentiment.

Rollin Daggett was at the time editor in chief of THE TERRITORIAL ENTERPRISE and Judge Charles C. Goodwin, who adored children and wrote verses of cloying sentimentality about "Pinkie," the infant daughter of Banker Blauvelt, was assistant. Outraged almost beyond coherence, Goodwin and Daggett forgathered over the bar in The Delta to plot revenge and imagine misfortune for the infamous Frank Leslies.

The calm before the storm lasted for some weeks and the Comstock had begun to forget all about the Leslie attack when reprisal arrived. On

COMSTOCK COMMOTION

Sunday, July 14, 1878, the entire front page of THE ENTERPRISE was devoted to an extended, documented, and damning exposure of the antecedents, personal habits, sex life, professional conduct, and lamentable moral character of Mr. and Mrs. Frank Leslie. Hardly a shred, fragment, or vestigial trace of reputation was left for the publishers of *Leslie's Illustrated Newspaper* to share between them.

Daggett and Goodwin, without disclosing to anyone in Virginia City their full intent, had retained a private detective in New York to investigate the affairs both domestic and professional of the Leslies. His findings, which had required months of undercover activity by several associated investigators, were reported anonymously but with such a wealth of documentation as to be essentially irrefutable.

The headline read:

OUR FEMALE SLANDERER

Mrs. Frank Leslie's Book Scandalizing the Families of Virginia City—The History of the Authoress—a Life Drama of Crime and Licentiousness—Startling Developments—etc., etc.

Mrs. Leslie, so deposed THE ENTERPRISE, was the probably illegitimate daughter of a rooming house proprietor "who let out rooms to single gentlemen by the day and no questions asked." Mrs. Leslie's first marriage to a David C. Peacock, it was stated, had been implemented with a shotgun. Her brother had committed suicide after an affair with Lola Montez, and her first husband, whom she had married "to gratify her taste for diamonds," had had their marriage annulled, and had died insane.

Shortly thereafter the former Mrs. Peacock and her mother, who by now seems to have been a partner in her daughter's love adventures, were set up in a "respectable district of New York City as lady and daughter of a retired gentleman who spent his time in Mobile." Patron of this arrangement was "a Congressman from Tennessee, the sort of man she was looking for as he had gold and precious stones . . . The lady in New York during his absence (in legislative halls) was more or less gay."

Next to appear in Mrs. Leslie's scandalous past was a "Mr. E. G. Squires . . . president of a railroad which gave him a large income and, withal, he was not married." The more or less gay lady gave the Tennessee lawgiver the gate and married Squires at Providence, Rhode Island, "the mother advising Providence to avoid any unpleasant talk or trouble which might be brought up in New York."

But hard luck stalked the future Mrs. Leslie. The railroad failed to earn its quarterly dividend, the president was obviously now very old hat indeed, and the question presented itself: how to be rid of the aged codger? Here Providence again intervened and Mrs. Squires made the acquaintance of an Englishman named Henry Carter who, under the name of Frank Leslie, was making a not inconsiderable success of *Leslie's Illustrated Newspaper*. A man of the world with useful connections, Leslie knew how to handle such matters. Squires was invited to "a grand dinner party in a disreputable house in West Twenty-Seventh Street"; champagne flowed in Niagaras and Squires was led off in front of a full quota of witnesses to a bedchamber by a professional courtesan named by THE ENTERPRISE investigator as "Gypsy." That was the end of the troublesome railroad business; Mrs. Squires was unopposed in her suit for divorce, and one year and two weeks later became Mrs. Frank Leslie.

"Now commenced a round of gayeties and extravagances," THE ENTERPRISE told its readers. "Leslie and his bride were to be found in all places where they could obtain admittance; but the doors of New York society were not open to them: there were some of the high toned who passed by on the other side of the way whenever they met." ·

In this delightful vein the front-page story in THE ENTERPRISE continued for five full columns of small type running 3,000 words to the column, and lest anyone should miss it in the daily edition of the paper, it was reprinted next day in its entirety in pamphlet form as a "Territorial Enterprise Extra" twenty-four pages in length, which is now one of the rarest of all items of Western Americana.

On its editorial page that triumphant Sunday, Daggett carried a single paragraph to point a moral in the miserable and by now disemboweled Frank Leslies. Under the heading of "A Strange Story," it read:

On the front page of *The Enterprise* this morning will be read the strange story of the Leslie family. It refers to Frank Leslie and his wife, the latter the author of a volume to which we have heretofore made reference entitled "A Pleasure Trip from Gotham to the Golden State" by Mrs. Frank Leslie. Desiring to learn something more of the life of a woman who in a spirit of malice so scandalized the wives and daughters of this city, we sent to New York for a history of the Leslie family and it has been furnished in detail. It is a terrible story of crime, heartlessness and immorality. But that the story is substantiated in the main by the records of the New York courts, it would read like a chapter of fiction. It is indeed a singular story and plainly explains the cause of the heartless assault of Mrs. Leslie upon the ladies of this coast.

Immediately following these elevating sentiments was a classified advertisement of THE ENTERPRISE editorial page: "Lost, at the Virginia &

Truckee depot or in its vicinity, a child's silver cup marked 'Baby.' Finder will be suitably rewarded by leaving same at Bob Patterson's International Saloon under the International Hotel."

Nevada's last formal duel had been fought only two years before the publication of THE ENTERPRISE exposé and it is conceivable that Daggett and Judge Goodwin might have been waited on by Leslie's seconds save for the circumstances that the magazine publisher's personal fortunes at about this time suffered severe reverses. He had overextended himself spectacularly, the property passed from his hands, and his extensive estates in New Jersey went on the block to satisfy creditors. It is doubtful if he had the carfare to come West with the idea of shooting up the editorial rooms in South C Street.

The legend of pistol-packing editors throughout the West's formative years had substantial foundation in fact. Mention has been made earlier of the remarkable aim of the *Rocky Mountain News*' William N. Byers.

Elsewhere in the howling wilderness beyond the wide Missouri editors fared worse than Sure-Shot Byers. The assassination of James King of William in San Francisco was a classic murder which touched off the activities of the famous Vigilance Committee. Another San Francisco editor, Edward Gilbert of the *Alta California*, was killed outright in a rifle duel with General J. W. Denver, for whom Denver City was shortly to be named, and the recollection of the event prevented his nomination by the Democratic party for President of the United States some years later. Charles de Young of the *San Francisco Chronicle* was fatally shot, before he could draw his own weapon, by a malcontent who, when he was acquitted, was drawn through the streets in a carriage to which a cheering mob attached themselves instead of horses.

In Denver, long after the smoke of these encounters had blown down the decades, Fred Bonfils and Harry Tammen, founders of the fortunes of the *Denver Post*, were both shot up and seriously wounded by a Missouri lawyer who was vexed by their abuse. The then governor of Colorado sent their assailant a note in jail: "I congratulate you upon your intention but must condemn your poor aim."

Tammen had been shot in the hips and was incandescent with rage. "Shot in the pants," he screamed. "The work of a fiend!"

Less successful than some of its feuds of earlier years was the attempt of one ENTERPRISE editor to do battle with the vested interest of the Comstock. The result was one of the shortest of all tenures of office by any editor in the paper's history, but it might be said that, though short of duration, Fred Hart's occupancy of the position was not devoid of merriment.

Few journalistic frontiersmen contributed so greatly to the original humor of Nevada as Frederick Hart, no relative of Bret Harte.

In the early 1870's, Hart, who worked on the *Reese River Reveille* as correspondent and later as editor, caused an international sensation with humorous sketches of frontier Nevada life. He wrote under the pseudonym of Van Jacquelin, and "whoppers" printed in the Austin paper by Hart were taken as literal truth by a German paper. His sprightly, Artemus-Ward style of writing, plus his handsome features and easygoing ways, won him the hearts of many Nevadans. After his term with the *Reveille*, Hart left his partner, John Booth, and compiled his sketches for publication. This book, extinct except for a few rare copies, was entitled *The Sazerac Lying Club* and was based on the activities of one of the liveliest groups in Austin.

For a short while, Hart worked on Gold Hill papers, and then friends secured for him the editorship of the Virginia City TERRITORIAL ENTERPRISE.

Hart had a genius for getting into trouble, and always with people a more prudent man would have cultivated assiduously. One of his first boners was a bitter editorial denouncing James G. Fair, at the moment running for office as United States Senator.

The editorial spoiled John Mackay's breakfast when he read it. On one of the few occasions remembered on the Lode when he completely lost his Irish temper, Mackay appeared without a hat at THE ENTERPRISE roaring that he owned half the paper, as he did indeed, and that no son of a bitch on his payroll was going to abuse his partner. From this remove it is difficult to imagine just what had motivated Hart to the folly of denouncing a man whose least whim could have him tossed into the gutter of C Street. Mackay was with difficulty restrained from taking a sledge hammer and smashing up the machinery that had printed the offending article.

Mackay was pacified and Hart was cautioned, but not for long. As Alf Doten delicately put it in an article for the *Nevada Magazine*, "Only a month later an east wind from the brewery struck Hart again, and under the resistless impulse he steered directly afoul of the Alta Mining Company, among the best patrons of THE ENTERPRISE."

Under the heading "The Alta Steal," Hart denounced the appropriation by the Alta Mining Company of the best resources of its neighbor, the Justice, as an act of piracy by the most abandoned gang of embezzlers ever allowed to operate outside prison walls. It was a masterpiece of invective and inspired imprudence.

Stockholders and executives in Alta at once started screaming for tar buckets and had at THE ENTERPRISE with doomsday screeches of grief and indignation. Hart, by now in the throes of a museum-piece hangover, heard the clattering tumbrels as they rolled down C Street. A glimpse through the parted curtains of his office at the gathering vigilantes told him that this time "the east wind from the brewery" had blown him no good whatsoever. He left by the back door as hard-rock miners from the Alta were securing a length of rope to the second-floor awning of THE ENTERPRISE and had begun beating down the doors, and caught the night cars out of Reno.

"His journalistic ship was wrecked forever, and he drifted about, picking up little jobs of reporting by way of precarious subsistence for a few months and finally, on August 30, 1897, died in the Sacramento County Hospital." So Judge Goodwin wrote Hart's obituary.

Their often untidy way of life considered, remarkably few editors of THE ENTERPRISE came to bad ends, most of them dying in bed surrounded by weeping and, in a few cases, expectant grandchildren. None even approximated the gaudy exit of T. S. Harris, publisher of the *Panamint News*, who, when that suburb of Hell (the phrase is Wells Fargo's) folded up, went to work on the staff of the *Los Angeles Evening Republican*. There, in a moment of vexation, he achieved the dream of every reporter since the beginning of time by shooting his own managing editor. He then wrote his own obituary: "I've had a hell of a time," and shot himself.

Most staff members, especially during the early years of the paper when pistol practice on the Comstock was constant and frequently deadly, escaped ventilation at the hands of outraged clients by narrow margins.

Gaslamps and Gunfire

No ROMAN emperor reigned in Nevada to lend grandeur to a golden age of letters, no open-handed Maecenas scattered patronage to seedy poets and needy playwrights, nor was there any magnificent Lorenzo to ease the lot of belles lettres.

The presiding genius of the Augustan age of sagebrush literature, had one been named for the role, would have been a profane little man in ruined whiskers wearing a soiled printer's apron with a typestick in his hand and a bottomless thirst for what his contemporaries were fond of calling "the ardent." For the great days of Nevada's literary flowering were also the golden age of the journeyman printer, the wicked, used-up, blasphemous, sodden, yet somehow reliable and atmospheric itinerant typesetter before the pestilence of Mergenthaler. He translated the copy of Sam Davis and Rollin Daggett, of Mark Twain and Wells Drury into the instant immortality of bourgeois and brevier, twelve ems to the column line.

He is gone now, the tramp printer in his hard derby hat who could quote "Lear" in its entirety and as often as not worked his cases with a Henry repeating rifle handy against the possibility of intrusion by Sioux or the opposition. He had stuck type for Sam Bowles on the *Springfield Republican* until the Sunday closing law of the Commonwealth made life intolerable for a free man, when he had gone to Albany to work for Thurlow Weed on the *Evening Journal*. There he had knocked a foreman down for doubting his string and boarded the steam cars for Omaha or Cincinnati or Little Rock. He had been working the day shift on the *Post-Dispatch* in St. Louis, setting one of John Cockerill's inflammatory editorials, for a fact, the day Colonel Alonzo Slayback had attempted to shoot Cockerill at his desk, but had misjudged his man and himself was carried to the street dead as muttons and leaking bourbon at every wound.

When the Southern Hotel burned he had set up the casualty list but the catastrophe was the greater for burning down Tony Faust's Oyster Saloon next door and he headed westward again. He ended his days sticking type for the *Free Press* at Bodie where a man had to be spry to

55

dodge the slugs that came through the walls at all hours, or at the long row of cases at the *California Alta,* or drinking with Dan De Quille in the Magnolia Saloon in Virginia City.

The nineteenth-century West knew a thousand tramp printers of note and disreputable pedigree: Thin Space Jones, Kid Glove Willie, Long Primer Fielding, Dirty Shirt Smith, and other notables perfumed with bourbon, who made history at the type cases of the *Deseret News, Tombstone Epitaph, Montana Register, Deadwood Times,* and the *Bad Lands Cowboy.* One of the most picturesque, as well as most literate of them all, was John Edward Hicks who later wrote his reminiscences in "Adventures of a Tramp Printer." On his first day of employment in the composing room of the first paper in Leavenworth, Kansas, Hicks' first editor was shot from under him, as it were, when he was assassinated in front of Pat Doran's saloon at the corner of Cherokee and Fifth streets.

In that summer of 1880 so many Kansas editors, publishers, and reporters were killed by gunfire in political and professional feuds that the *Kansas City Times,* in a pre–Roy Roberts age of plains journalism, suggested that a specimen Kansas country editor be stuffed and preserved in a museum before the race became altogether extinct. "It is only a question of whether a Leavenworth editor dies by whisky or powder," said the *Times.* "The powder, generally being of better quality than the whisky, usually accomplishes its end first."

The road of the tramp printer in those days was wild and free, and wandering type slingers forgathered in a score of Skid Roads, Barbary Coasts, Pi Alleys, Humbug Squares, and Hell's Half Acres to pass the bottle while exchanging monstrosities of mendacity and singing "The E-I-Ree Was Rising" and "Down in the Lehigh Valley." They exchanged reminiscences of Denver in the early Cherry Creek days and the time when Opie Read was setting the columns of the *Arkansas Traveler.* Their world was as well defined and populated with figures of legend as the worlds of the horse traders, stage drivers, medicine men, itinerant preachers, and strolling Shakespeareans, who were their contemporaries.

Now the tramp printer is with the ages, forever a part of the folklore of a departed time in a younger America.

In the golden age of THE ENTERPRISE the bond between the editorial side and the mechanical department was strong. In its earliest days, editor and compositor had been one and the same, and Jernegan took typestick in hand to set Jernegan's leaders and locked them in the chases of the press owned by Jernegan. In metropolitan news plants today staff writers seldom know the name or size of the type in which their copy is set and makeup is supervised by a specialist who serves as a sort of adjutant or liaison man between editorial and composing rooms.

Such was not always the arrangement.

Both Joe Goodman and Dennis McCarthy were printers before they were ever editor and publisher, and many ENTERPRISE editors who followed them were fully as at home at the type cases as they were with the subjunctive. Some, more so. Jonathan Williams, whose copy had been "licked into shape" by his printers, is a good example. So close was the relationship between reporter and compositor that as long as they were on Goodman's staff, Mark Twain and Dan De Quille wrote at a deal table in the press room in preference to using desks upstairs, and De Quille held to the practice as long as he lived.

One spring day in 1873 a sixteen-year-old tramp printer went to work for Goodman in the still standing red-brick offices in South C Street. He lost his first week's salary, about $40, playing faro in Gentry & Crittenden's, and kicked himself all the way down the Geiger Grade for being a sucker. He was Fremont Older, later the grand old man of San Francisco letters, and between Virginia City and the Golden Gate he paused briefly to become foreman of a job plant in Reno; he never bet on the turn of a card again.

Ivory towers were few and far between in the American West. Beautiful letters almost invariably had to be translated into pork chops and rent; and this, together with the universally admitted affinity of printer's ink for whisky, strongly conditioned the literature of the time. Without any exception worth the naming, all Nevada literature of the nineteenth century was the literature of journalism. Every writer one can name in the time and place wrote for a newspaper or other periodical, even though he might eventually achieve the dignity of boards.

The first and some of the best of all reporting of the Nevada scene was that of J. Ross Browne for *Harper's Monthly*. Fred Hart, whose tales of the Sazerac Lying Club were to become classics, wrote variously for the *Reese River Reveille*, the *Hamilton Evening Telegram*, and THE TERRITORIAL ENTERPRISE. Sam Davis' genius for local history found its outlet in the *Carson Appeal* and all of the best of De Quille originally appeared in THE ENTERPRISE. The list is endless and almost definitive. Nevada letters, first and last, were Nevada newspaper stories.

One of the itinerant printers who made periodical stops in the composing room of THE ENTERPRISE in its early days was Colonel James Townsend. The "Colonel," as in the case of Colonel Abe Curry, was honorary and Townsend was known well and universally in the West as Lying Jim. Lying Jim had arrived in San Francisco aboard a Boston clipper in the early days of the gold rush and came to THE ENTERPRISE shortly after the paper's own advent on the Comstock. He both wrote copy for the paper and set it in type, and in an age when half the stories in any edition might well be suspect as a hoax, his hoaxes were characterized by such plausibility as to fool even his intimates.

Lying Jim once invented in THE ENTERPRISE a windmill for lifting sand and gravel, a sort of primitive example of today's earth-moving machinery, that had learned engineers figuring out its horsepower and capacity in cubic yards per diem. Even in the 'sixties there were cynics around Virginia City who scoffed at Mark Twain's claim to creating his celebrated jumping frog of Calaveras and who said that Lying Jim had been telling the story for years before Clemens ever appeared on the scene or began calling himself Mark Twain.

Fremont Older, who himself had served as a compositor for Goodman, fondly recalled a tramp printer named Babbitt in his reminiscences. Babbitt wrote and spoke both French and German fluently, but drank so much that even when not positively in wine he staggered noticeably. He would start for a door and miss it by two or three feet; a staircase presented a definite occupational hazard.

One day he appeared at THE ENTERPRISE gorgeously arrayed in new and fashionable gentleman's apparel, including a silk top hat on which the lure had just been lovingly laid. Babbitt was as boiled as his shirt front.

"Where did you get the new raiment?" asked Older. "And the load?"

"I got the clothes on tick at Roos Brothers just across the street by telling Mr. Roos my story in French," said the printer. "He was so moved by my plight that he trusted me. The jag I got from the barkeep at the Hoffbrau. I told him my story in German and he was so touched by my plight that he trusted me. I'm now going down to the International where the headwaiter thinks I'm a correspondent for Frank Leslie who'll get his name in the next issue of the paper and get a venison dinner on the cuff."

Babbitt was a fellow of revolting appearance, hollow-chested, stoop-shouldered, and religiously opposed to washing. He was last heard of headed for Winnemucca, where he was to be the picture groom of a young schoolma'am. He had courted her by mail, thoughtfully enclosing as a clincher the photograph of a handsome faro dealer from Crittenden's.

TIME OUT FOR PISMOS AND PISCO

THE TRAMP PRINTER of tradition was a familiar Comstock character in the great days of THE ENTERPRISE. Chapman's Chop House in North B Street, which kept open all night, was a favored resort for the fraternity of the cases, for here, in moments of economic desperation, Pismo clams and Pisco punches could be carried on the cuff until payday. The frock coat and top hat were occupational attire, to be followed in a later generation by the short walking tailcoat and cast-iron derby.

Judge Goodwin, who came to THE ENTERPRISE staff long after Mark Twain had departed for the great world beyond Nevada, admired him with moderation and ascribed what he admired in him to the influence of Goodman. The judge recalls that after the celebrated holdup of Twain on the Divide and the lifting of his watch by a group of friends headed by George Birdsall, the author decided to go down below to San Francisco for a week end and Birdsall returned the watch to him as he was sitting in a California Company stage in front of the International Hotel.

"It's all very well for you to return my property," said Clemens in his characteristic drawl. "But you performed far too professionally to be mere amateurs at highway robbery. What did you do with the $25,000 you took from Wells Fargo's coach on the Geiger Grade last week?"

When he finally achieved San Francisco on this occasion Clemens was just in time for one of California's periodic earthquakes—which came on a Sunday morning—and he wrote a description of the event for THE ENTERPRISE. Although the file containing it exists nowhere, Judge Goodwin was able to quote parts of it verbatim many years later:

When the earthquake came on Sunday morning [Mark Twain wrote] there was but one man in San Francisco who showed any presence of mind and he was over in Oakland. He did just what I thought of doing and would have done had I had any opportunity—he went down out of his pulpit and embraced a woman. The newspapers said it was his wife. Maybe it was, but if so it was a pity. It would have shown so much more presence of mind if he had embraced some other gentleman's wife.

A young man came down from the fifth story of a house on Stockton Street with no clothing except a sort of knitted undershirt which came as near to concealing his person as the foil on its neck does a champagne bottle. Men shouted to him, little boys yelled at him, and women besought him to take their sun bonnets, their aprons, their hoopskirts, anything in the world to cover himself up and not stand there distracting people's attention from the earthquake. He looked all around and then looked down at himself, and then he went upstairs. I am told he went up lively.

Pete Hopkins was shaken off Telegraph Hill and on his way down landed on a three-story brick house (he weighed 430 pounds) and the papers, always misrepresenting things, ascribed the destruction of the house to the earthquake.

To the generation in which it was written this was newspaper writing to provoke cascades of inextinguishable merriment.

Clemens' *cursus honorum* on THE ENTERPRISE closely followed the still accepted progress of writers on any metropolitan newspaper of prudent and ordered professional ways. He began at the bottom as a district man, or stringer, came to the home office to serve as local reporter on the city staff,

REPORTER IN THE GREAT TRADITION

WRITING UNDER the pen name of Dan De Quille, William Wright
was for thirty years reporter and mining editor of THE TERRITORIAL EN-
TERPRISE in its golden years. His friendship and example are credited
with having greatly shaped the peculiar genius of Mark Twain.

moved upward to write occasional features as differentiated from straight news, and finally achieved the status of a recognized by-liner as drama reviewer.

His first connection with THE ENTERPRISE was as its correspondent in Aurora in the Esmeralda diggings, ninety-odd miles to the south of Virginia City and, at the time, a mining camp of importance. Shortly thereafter Aurora declined into borrasca and most of its inhabitants drifted to the neighboring town of Bodie, celebrated in Western legend and in proper fact as the wickedest of all frontier communities and home port of "the bad man from Bodie" of later fame.

So untidy was Bodie's social life that Nevada folklore tells of the small daughter of a miner who was removing there from Aurora to seek employment in the North Noonday Mine who, when she said her prayers the last night before leaving, prayed "Good-by, God! We're going to Bodie." The impious *Bodie Free Press*, reveling in the town's riotous fame, said the quotation had been improperly punctuated and should read, "Good! By God, we're going to Bodie!"

Clemens and his brother Orion, prospecting in the Esmeralda and filing dispatches to Virginia City, occasionally went over to Bodie for the week end to visit with friends on the staffs of the *Free Press* and *Standard* and to keep their hand in as printers. Until comparatively recently there was, kicking around in near-by Bridgeport, a hand press locally known as "Mark Twain press" which had reportedly seen service in Bodie in the 'sixties. Built under an 1860 patent by Morgan & Wilcox Manufacturing Company of Middletown, New York, the press was upright with a crank-and-belt controlled retractable carriage to accommodate the chases, and is now in the Denver Art Museum.

After a night or two of the company to be found in the Bodie House, Parole Saloon, The Senate, and the Philadelphia Brewery, Fairfield's stage would transport the brothers Clemens, pale and twitching, back to Aurora.

It required a minimum of adjustment when Joe Goodman sent for Clemens to come to the home office to replace a regular staff member, William Wright, who signed his articles Dan De Quille and who had gone back to Iowa "in the states" to visit his family. Virginia City's night life was similar in character to that of Bodie except where improvements had been devised. There were by now, for example, more than one hundred saloons where Bodie had boasted but a quarter that number. There were murders by the score and bloody scuffles past all counting. It was a good place for a police reporter to practice his special expertise.

"Can you use a revolver?" was the first question asked Wells Drury by Alf Doten the day he reported to work on the *Gold Hill News*. It was as conventional an inquiry as asking today's new man if he can write cable-ese or do rewrite. Drury's first assignment that same day was to cover a shooting over the Divide in Virginia City, where he viewed the remains of John Dalley, killed by Dick Carter, a case keeper for Tom Buckner's faro game in the Sawdust Corner. Wells was of a mind that it was the prettiest gunshot wound he had ever seen.

Clemens complained that on his first day on duty for THE ENTERPRISE there hadn't been any violence worth a stick of space in the paper. This was probably one of his most triumphant understatements, and in any event was soon to be rectified, for 1863 was to prove the most deplorable in Comstock history from the viewpoint of violence, and 1863 was only four months off when Clemens made his statement.

The Virginia City in which THE TERRITORIAL ENTERPRISE found itself established in the early 'sixties was the archetype of the tumults and lawlessness that characterized all the mining towns of the Old West in greater or less degree. No full record of the crimes of violence has survived, and those that were kept could hardly be expected to encompass the innumerable departures from conventional decorum which marked almost every tick of the clock along the length and breadth of the Comstock Lode.

The year of THE ENTERPRISE' arrival from Carson City witnessed some of the more atrocious murders in Virginia City's long record of bloodshed, among them the assassination of Homer Woodruff by Sam Brown, a professional thug and gunman, and the hilarious shooting of a Mexican in Light's saloon, in which Bill Burns and Jeff Standifer each claimed the honor of having fired the fatal shot. The argument lasted for several days and sold a great deal of conversational whisky at Light's.

The year 1863, however, by which time THE ENTERPRISE was established as a connoisseur of sudden and violent death, was a banner year in the annals of assault, mayhem, murder, and, of course, acquittal in Virginia City. A partial list of the departed whose names achieved a brief immortality in the local news columns of THE ENTERPRISE would include William Jones, who was stabbed to death by an unknown assailant just inside the frosted glass doors of the Texas Saloon; Police Officers John Reed and John McMahon, who were shot and killed in a gun battle with a man named Campbell in North C Street, with Campbell's inevitable acquittal on grounds of self-defense; the discovery of the body of one Kelly, first name unknown, who had been carved up into steaks and chops

Death Any Afternoon

Execution of John Millain, for the Murder of Julia Bulette.

Most stylish social function of the Comstock's early years was the hanging, at eighteen minutes before one o'clock, April 24, 1868, of John Millain, a personable Frenchman implicated in the murder the previous year of Julia Bulette, Virginia City's first and easily most publicized courtesan. A full municipal holiday was declared for the occasion and THE TERRITORIAL ENTERPRISE, members of whose staff were specially invited guests on the scaffold, reported the event next day in three full columns of better than 4,000 words. The *California Police Gazette* next week printed it in full, together with the woodcut shown here. The starred performer in the ceremony arrived in an open barouche accompanied by Father (later Bishop) Manogue and followed by other rented hacks bearing the sheriff of Storey County and state dignitaries, all wearing top hats and frock coats. The national guard and specially deputized citizens armed with repeating rifles maintained order among a crowd of 5,000, also in holiday mood and attire. The crowd roared as the trap was sprung and then streamed back to town to purchase seats for Piper's Opera, where a special treat was promised for that evening. Mark Twain was to lecture on his adventures in the Holy Land.

Highlife Any Evening

Editors in the outside world were well aware of the compelling fascination of a Virginia City date line and never failed to give their readers the fullest details of the Comstock's countless shootings, stabbings, horsewhippings, duels, suicides, and other excursions into the field of violence. Usually an exchange copy of THE ENTER-PRISE was the handiest guide to the most recent and florid tumults in Washoe. Never a newspaper to miss the fun, the *California Police Gazette*, a cheerful feuilleton published weekly in San Francisco, could always be relied on to have the latest and most un-tranquil news from C Street, often illustrated with a realistic wood-cut such as the one below depicting "A Lively Row at the National Brewery, in Virginia City, Nevada." The *Gazette* had a picture file of ten woodcuts, mostly devoted to such heady matters as this, which it used in rotation with a new caption as occasion demanded. *Gazette* readers reacted most favorably to pictures captioned: "It is my husband! Go by the window and quickly!" or "Stand, Sir, or I will pistol you for a coward!" Today the *California Police Gazette* is one of the rarest of all items of Californiana and only a slender file reposes in the vaults of the Bancroft Library.

A Lively Row at the National Brewery, in Virginia City, Nevada.

in a C Street cellar by party or parties unknown; and the regrettable death at the hands of Joe McGee of the proprietor of the San Francisco Saloon at the corner of B and Union streets, a site afterward occupied for more cultural ends by Piper's Opera.

In August, J. P. Cullen was sentenced to two and a half years in the state prison at Carson for slaughtering a companion over a game of cards and the sentence, Thompson & West note, was considered barbarously severe. John Dennis, alias Eldorado Johnny, was shot and killed in a South C Street tavern by Langford Peel, better known as Farmer Peel, who himself came to no good end a few years later in Montana. Yuk Lee was shot and killed by another unidentified Chinaman on the Ophir Road out of Gold Hill and one wonders that such an inconsequential matter got into the record at all. Sugar Foot Jack Merrill was shot and killed in the middle of C Street by an assailant who thoughtfully ran through The Delta and out the back door before the law could arrive. Charles Steer was shot and killed for using abusive language about Deborah Phillips, a prostitute, and Deborah got a year in the gow which Governor Nye abated to five months; James Dodd was mortally ventilated by Daniel Farney for attempting to stop a dog fight in a Gold Hill saloon and the jury agreed that anyone who attempted to spoil a sporting event deserved to be eliminated; Jack Butler was shot, in places too numerous for the coroner to count, by his mistress, a forthright girl known as Sailor Jack, whom a chivalrous jury promptly acquitted by acclaim. And, to round out the year with lethal finality and a fine feeling for panache, Joe McGee was shot and killed down at Carson City with the same gun with which, just a year before to the day, he had given his quietus to Jack Williams, a notorious desperado, during the course of a faro game in Pat Lynch's Saloon.

An example of the unpredictability of life in Virginia City even as late as the mid-'seventies is the story of Jim Orndorff and Jack McGee (no relative of the unfortunate Joe of a decade previous) who were joint proprietors of the Delta Saloon where editorial conference of THE ENTERPRISE is held to this day. The premises were celebrated for decorous conduct; in many years there was never a serious brawl in The Delta. This tranquil interregnum came to an abrupt end when, in a single evening, Orndorff was shot and killed while ejecting an abusive customer and McGee was murdered by his mistress.

Long after gunfighting had disappeared elsewhere in the West firearms played a part in life in Virginia City. Assassinations and gun duels flourished, to the amazement of observers, in a community where evening dress, organized society, and the refinements of urban life were an accepted pattern of life. It gave the town a name for animation which it has never entirely lost.

Well could Maxfield, the Comstock's foremost funeral director, afford space to advertise his wares and service in the following elegant terms:

A LARGE ASSORTMENT OF

MAHOGANY AND METALLIC COFFINS,

LEAD COFFINS, SHROUDS, COLLARS, CRAVATS,

SILVER COFFIN PLATES, GRAVE STONES

ETC., CONSTANTLY ON HAND.

HEARSES and COACHES, together with every variety of FUNERAL EQUIP-MENTS, furnished to order.

Especial attention given to DISINTERRING BODIES, and preparing them for Shipment to the Atlantic States and elsewhere.

IRON AND WOOD GRAVE INCLOSURES

— AND —

MARBLE TOMB STONES,

FURNISHED TO ORDER.

Senior editor of THE TERRITORIAL ENTERPRISE when Clemens arrived dusty and disheveled from his trip across the Nevada desert was Dan De Quille. Over De Quille's desk went his first copy and it was from the older man (De Quille was Clemens' senior by six years) that the future Mark Twain learned the technique of humorous writing which was eventually to gain him world fame.

De Quille was already a past master at the perpetration of newspaper hoaxes which embraced the description of imaginary catastrophes, the evolution of straw men as enemies, and, most of all, the pseudoscientific fabrication of remarkable natural wonders or marvels of invention fobbed off on a credulous world. De Quille had already launched his celebrated story of "The Traveling Stones of Pahranagat Valley," which were supposed to be controlled by mysterious electric impulses which alternately attracted them to a central focal point and then redistributed them to distant parts of the landscape in a fetching geologic pavane.*

All Nevada was gratified when the story reached Germany and a group of learned scientists was thrown into ecstasies of wonderment by the rolling stones. They addressed respectful inquiries to the Hochvolgeboren Herr Doktor Dan De Quille, the eminent physicist of Virginiastadt, and were with only the greatest difficulty persuaded that the story was woven from whole cloth and constituted something very funny in the lexicon of American humor. The scientists of Bonn pulled their whiskers thoughtfully and turned to other matters.

De Quille and Clemens hit it off from the start and shortly shared rooms together in a house in North B Street across from the site today of Piper's Opera. Their hours were identical, their professional preoccupation the same. They shared a common appreciation of sly hoorah and spent hours together emptying bottles which had originally been filled in Bourbon County, Kentucky.

Inevitably the impressionable Clemens must become the author of one of The Enterprise' by now celebrated hoaxes. Although the Civil War was raging in the East and threats and plots of secession were alarming California and the Comstock itself, the Overland telegraph brought all too scanty dispatches of the epic struggle and the paper's bedsheet pages must be filled with local news of a readable and interesting nature. By convention, the third page was assigned as space for all stories of a purely personal authorship by members of the local staff and here under the nom de plume Josh there shortly appeared the burlesque of the petrified man.

This first of Clemens' many similar canards was aimed at ridiculing a Nevadan to whom he seemed to take a professional dislike, Judge G. T. Sewell, Justice of the Peace and Coroner of the Humboldt Mining District, which was and is located at prudent remove from Virginia City. The

---

* Hoaxes were not by any means confined to the rowdy newspapers of the youthful West. In New York on November 9, 1874, James Gordon Bennett's *Herald* startled its Sunday readers with the alarming intelligence that during the night a widespread delivery had been effected among the wild animals in the Central Park Zoo and that the park itself was crawling with ferocious lions, tigers, and panthers. Good citizens were summoned by the mayor to come armed, at once, and assemble at the Fifty-ninth Street entrance to assist the police and militia in shooting the beasts. With a variety of armament New Yorkers arrived by thousands, only to find the animals in their cages where they belonged. The next day Whitelaw Reid's *New York Tribune* took a stuffy view of the affair, characterizing it as "a puerile invention distressing to many people . . . a ghastly effort at fun which should justify a prompt entry into the Tombs for its author."

Josh story told of the discovery thereabout of the remains of a petrified pioneer who had been dead for 300 years and over whose remains the magistrate solemnly held inquest. Judge Sewell decided that he had perished of "protracted exposure" and the tenor of the story generally suggested that the man of law was at once pompous and witless.

Clemens was bitterly disappointed when Sewell failed to rise to the lure and was even reported to have laughed heartily at the caricature of his officiousness, but like De Quille's rolling stones, the hoax was widely reprinted and, like the marvel of Pahranagat Valley, it attracted the attention of august personages far beyond the rim of Nevada's world. *The Lancet* of London, irreproachable medical journal of science and apparently irreproachably humorless, mentioned the discovery professionally and Clemens felt better.

Twain's most celebrated of all hoaxes and one which did the reputation of THE ENTERPRISE no special good was a singularly tasteless mendacity known as "The Empire City Massacre." The bloody account, printed in THE ENTERPRISE with a wealth of substantiating detail, told how wholesale murder had been committed by one "P. Hopkins or Philip Hopkins" at Empire, the stamp-mill city near Carson, where he had slaughtered his wife and seven children, maimed two others, severed his wife's head from the corpse, and then hastened to Carson City to cut his own throat and fall dead on the sidewalk in front of the Magnolia Saloon. As his informant of the affair Mark named Old Abe Curry, Carson's first citizen and patriarch, and he assigned the blame for Hopkins' fatal derangement on unfortunate speculation in Comstock mining properties on the strength of reports in San Francisco papers. "It is presumed that this misfortune drove him mad and resulted in his killing his family."

To Nevadans familiar with its geographic locale the story was transparently a hoax. Philip Hopkins, owner of The Magnolia, was notoriously unmarried; there were no pine woods at Empire such as were mentioned in the story, and other flagrant inconsistencies should have earmarked it to any thinking person as a monumental fabrication in bad taste.

So sensational, however, was the nature of the story and so realistic its horrid details that the *Gold Hill News* promptly lifted it for its own editions and the account received wide credence in California where its fakements were not readily perceived.

THE ENTERPRISE printed a signed retraction the next day, but the rest of the Comstock press joined the *News* in bitterly denouncing the affair for its shockingly bad taste, and its intended satire at the expense of dishonest mining editors in San Francisco was altogether overlooked in the uproar. "The Empire City Massacre" marked the high tide of the newspaper hoax so far as THE ENTERPRISE was concerned, and thereafter the practice was frowned upon by the management with great frowning.

Throughout the entire Civil War THE ENTERPRISE complained that news of the conflict was hard to come by. Its New York correspondence was from Horace Greeley's revered *New York Tribune*, and Goodman shared heartily in the influential Eastern paper's championing of Lincoln and the Union Cause.

Not until after hostilities ceased could telegraphic sources supply enough news of the world to satisfy THE ENTERPRISE, and when the tide reversed itself the Comstock's leading daily was deluged with feature material for which it had neither use nor space.

"A pressure of Eastern telegraphic news, much of it of little importance, but all claiming a place in full through habitual indulgence compels us to omit considerable matter prepared for other departments," THE ENTERPRISE complained in its issue of June 29, 1869. "For the past three or four months the telegraphic news reporters of the East have vied with one another in the transmission of trash over the wires, and if they do not use a little more discretion hereafter we shall substitute advertisements for their contradictory squabble."

The intimation that the paper was leaving out advertising that might well have run to its profit in favor of foreign news will come as a revelation to modern business offices.

Gaining in assurance under the guiding influence of De Quille, Clemens was assigned to cover the sessions of the Nevada Legislature at Carson City when the lawgivers assembled in 1863. The Sagebrush Capital was beginning to take on overtones of metropolis. No longer did the solons journey between town and the Hot Springs via the primeval railroad of Colonel Abe Curry. State officials in glossy top hats and broadcloth sipped French champagne of an evening in a multiplicity of decorous bars that were replacing the barrel houses of THE ENTERPRISE' Carson interlude. Clemens was statehouse reporter for the most influential paper in the commonwealth and his feuds began to take on loftier aspects than mere hayseed hassles with dunghill magistrates.

He picked a professional quarrel with the statehouse man for the *Virginia City Union*, Clement Rice, whom he saluted in his own dispatches to the Comstock as "The Unreliable." Rice saw the promotional possibilities of feud and had at Clemens with a variety of insults accumulated over a lifetime of political reporting. The two met on the best of terms over the gentlemen's bar at the Ormsby House after dinner and assailed each other with cleavers and meat axes in next morning's editions. Clemens' fame as author of the Josh dispatches became something more than merely local. He was becoming the butcher boy of the brevier.

In 1863 Mark Twain as a figure of American letters was born.

For reasons of his own, Clemens acquired a distaste for the by-line Josh and in February of 1863 he signed his first dispatch from Carson City to THE ENTERPRISE with the pen name that was destined for immortality: Mark Twain.

Many conflicting reports were circulated as to his choice of the name and Clemens himself was finally forced, some fourteen years later, to correct them in a letter to the *Daily Alta California*. It explained that the name had originated with Captain Isaiah Sellers, a friend of Clemens' Mississippi steamboating days, who had signed it to various ships' news items which appeared in the *New Orleans Picayune*. Sellers had recently died (his grave can be seen to this day at St. Louis, showing his marble likeness in full navigator's uniform) and Clemens "had laid violent hands on it without asking permission of the proprietor's remains."

Ninety years later the inheritors of THE TERRITORIAL ENTERPRISE' fortunes were fond of referring to their property upon occasion as "the literary birthplace of Mark Twain."

Rejoicing in the distinction of a widely admired nom de plume, Mark Twain's political dispatches began to acquire more character than they had previously possessed, although their humor could by no stretch of the imagination be described as subtle. Witness an account written for THE ENTERPRISE in December 1863 under a Washoe City date line:

> CARSON, MIDNIGHT
> December 23d.

EDS., *Enterprise:*

On the last night of the session, Hon. Thomas Hannah announced that a Grand Bull Drivers' Convention would assemble in Washoe City, on the 22d, to receive Hon. Jim Sturtevant and the other members of the Washoe delegation. I journeyed to the place yesterday to see that the ovation was properly conducted I traveled per stage. The Unreliable of the *Union* went also—for the purpose of distorting the facts. The weather was delightful. It snowed the entire day. The wind blew such a hurricane that the coach drifted sideways from one toll road to another, and sometimes utterly refused to mind her helm. It is a fearful thing to be at sea in a stagecoach. We were anxious to get to Washoe by four o'clock, but luck was against us; we were delayed by stress of weather; we were

71

hindered by the bad condition of the various toll roads; we finally broke the after spring of the wagon, and had to lay up for repairs. Therefore we only reached Washoe at dusk. Messrs. Lovejoy, Howard, Winters, Sturtevant, and Speaker Mills had left Carson ahead of us, and we found them in the city. They had not beaten us much, however, as I could perceive by their upright walk and untangled conversation. At 6 P.M., the Carson City Brass Band, followed by the Committee of Arrangements, and the Chairman of the Convention, and the delegation, and the invited guests, and the citizens generally, and the hurricane, marched up one of the most principal streets, and filed in imposing procession into Foulke's Hall. The delegation, and the guests, and the band, were provided with comfortable seats near the Chairman's desk, and the constituency occupied the body-pews. The delegation and the guests stood up and formed a semi-circle, and Mr. Gregory introduced them one at a time to the constituency. Mr. Gregory did this with much grace and dignity, albeit he affected to stammer and gasp, and hesitate, and look colicky, and miscall the names, and miscall them again by way of correcting himself, and grab desperately at invisible things in the air—all with a charming pretense of being scared . . .

The Chairman, Mr. Gaston, introduced Colonel Howard, and that gentleman addressed the people in his peculiarly grave and dignified manner. The constituency gave way to successive cataracts of laughter, which was singularly out of keeping with the stern seriousness of the speaker's bearing. He spoke about ten minutes, and then took his seat, in spite of the express wish of the audience that he should go on. . . .

Mark Twain, by the end of 1863, was a recognized character around Washoe and Carson City, on speaking terms with territorial dignitaries and politicians. The stage, through the local agency of Maguire's Opera House in D Street, opened to him vistas of potentiality in the great world outside of Nevada in which, eventually, his peculiar genius was to find recognition.

Maguire had completed his Opera only a short time previous and its gorgeous interior was the wonder of Washoe. A double tier of boxes flanked its spacious stage; their chairs were upholstered in red plush. The curtain depicted Lake Tahoe at sunset in a profusion of color that would have amazed William Turner, the English painter and himself a connoisseur of sunsets. The rails were swathed in red velvet and red velvet cords across the aisles separated the boxholding elect from the many. Glittering chandeliers of French crystal hung from the ceiling and there was a vast Turkey carpet on the floor. Handsome and useful spittoons replaced the accustomed sawdust.

The concessions in the lobby included a billiard room, smoking parlors and cigar stands, a farobank layout, and a sumptuous gentlemen's bar inlaid with genuine ivory.

GASLAMPS AND GUNFIRE

Opening night had been characterized by drama not on the program printed on silk playbills at THE ENTERPRISE job plant. Two gamblers on bad terms had found themselves seated in stage boxes directly opposite each other and the opportunity for pranging someone was irresistible. At one and the same instant Colt's dragoon revolvers appeared from under the tails of broadcloth frock coats and the auditorium was filled with the flash and bang of black powder. Bits of gilt woodwork flew in splinters; holes forty-five one-hundredths of an inch in diameter appeared in the plaster. Women screamed prettily and gentlemen in adjacent boxes regretted that their own evening attire had not included firearms along with their diamond shirt studs and ribboned watch fobs.

In the end, when the contestants, as yet unscathed, paused to reload, Maguire's ushers threw them out of the theater and the curtain was rung up on Julia Dean Hayne and Walter Leman in Bulwer-Lytton's "Money," fresh from a triumphant run at the Haymarket Theater in London, England.

In its early years Maguire's stage knew the presence of, and his four sheets throughout the Lode carried the magic names of Edwin Booth, Lola Montez, Lotta Crabtree, and Helena Modjeska. Later, Maguire's successor, Piper's Opera was to be world-celebrated for its performances by Joe Jefferson, May Robson, E. H. Sothern, Salvini the Younger, Lillian Russell, and Maude Adams. Only a few years from now Mark Twain was himself to be billed as a stellar attraction at Piper's. He delivered his lecture on the Holy Land against strong competition, since it was scheduled the same day that John Millain was hanged for the murder of Julia Bulette.

A ranking name in the entertainment world of the decade was that of Artemus Ward. His humor as a monologist was earthy and understandable to a generation of Americans whose experiences were of the soil and crossroads townships removed from the sophistications of urbanity. Actually Ward was educated, well-spoken, and a man of the world, but he cultivated a rustic approach and seedy appearance on the platform.

Maguire, always alert for attractions to fill his commodious new Opera, had sent a message to Ward in New York City asking what he would take for one hundred nights, and Washoe dissolved in merriment at his reply, "Brandy and soda!" Since then Ward had gone on to even bigger things, impersonating on the stage a traveling showman closely resembling Phineas Barnum and romping through the evening with a fast patter of puns, double takes, and more or less inspired buffoonery. He laid them in the aisles with his description of Virginia City "set in the midst of a great desert—a wild moor——like Othello."

The advent of Artemus Ward at Virginia City was one of the high points in Mark Twain's life. As had been the case with Dan De Quille, the two men, both celebrities in their own right, struck up an instant friendship. His first appearance at Maguire's was the performance of what he called "Babes in the Woods." The title was meaningless, but Twain in the row of seats reserved for members of THE ENTERPRISE staff (this was before the War of the Four Roses between Maguire and the newspaper) was convulsed with Ward's funeral attire, melancholy face, and deadpan delivery. After the performance Twain was introduced to Ward at what turned out to be a Field of the Cloth of Sawdust in Jacob Reim's saloon.

Ward's itinerary called for three appearances at Maguire's before moving on to the next stand in San Francisco. He stayed three weeks, to participate in one of the most celebrated binges in the history of the Comstock where binges of a major order were commonplace.

The compelling fascination which the Nevada desert, in spectacular contrast to the luxurious devisings of life within stone's throw of the sagebrush wasteland, held for Artemus Ward was to be almost precisely paralleled half a century later by another actor, Nat Goodwin, at Goldfield. Goodwin arrived in the last of the Nevada bonanzas to play at the Hippodrome Theater and was so delighted with the hospitality of the place that he abandoned his road tour to become associated with the boom on a semipermanent basis.

Artemus Ward associated himself with the staff of THE ENTERPRISE in a definitive project to take the Comstock apart and see what made it tick.

His stay at Maguire's was prolonged indefinitely and Maguire was delighted, since Ward had captured the fancy of the miners and many returned night after night to applaud his act. When the show was over a delegation of ENTERPRISE staffmen, almost invariably headed by Mark Twain and Dan De Quille, waited at the stage door to show him the elephant.

One night they would adjourn to Chauvel's, next door to the Medan Building, for sage hen and champagne in a private dining room to escape the importunities of admirers drinking in the front bar. Thence they would make the rounds, passing the time of morning with Joe Loryea, proprietor of Almack's, and going on to bigger and better things, their train augmented by casual encounters, to The Old Corner, The Bank Exchange, and

Whitehall, all located within two city blocks of each other in a concentration of convenience not even to be duplicated in New York in the age of the Girl from Rector's. As often as not they would end the evening long after the sun had come up Six Mile Canyon, in a steam room at Moritz's Bath House ("Baths—Bains—Banos" it advertised in all current languages), at No. 6 North B Street at no great remove from Clemens' lodgings and just up the street from the side entry to the International where Ward was staying.

Late that afternoon they would meet for a refreshing eye-opener or phlegm-cutter at the Fashion, followed by eggs Vienna to stay the inner man and get Ward through his performance.

Their nocturnal itinerary was available to almost limitless variations. Supper would be at Barnum's and the ports of call thereafter would follow a dizzy routing through the Grayhound Saloon, the Young America, Pat Bell's place, and The Delta, ending with *cafe espresso* from a wonderfully complicated machine, all nickel and faucets and gauges, back of the bar at Adolph Kuhnhaeser's German Coffee Saloon in North B.

One night they were drinking sociable-like with Isaac Brokaw, foreman of Virginia City Engine Company No. 1 and the town's social arbiter, at John Piper's Old Corner Saloon when a pistol-waving ruffian weaved up to Ward and shoved a Colt's Navy against his flowered waistcoat, with a demand for excerpts from "Babes in the Woods." Confronted with *force majeur*, Ward obliged and the bad man, enchanted with the command performance, set drinks up for everyone and led a cheer for "that great poetical poet, William W. Shakespeare."

Contemporary report of the splendid exchanges on these occasions may not do entire justice to the brilliant character of the participants. Once Clemens is reported to have risen to propose a toast with the ringing words, "I give you Upper Canada!" "Why," asked Ward on cue, "do you give me Upper Canada?" "Because I don't want it!"

This sort of thing carried a man far in the Comstock 'sixties.

At length, like all good things, Ward's stay in Virginia City approached its end. It was just as well. The staff of THE ENTERPRISE was beginning to show signs of wear and Mark Twain's holograph copy was at times illegible even to compositors who had become skilled in their profession deciphering the turkey tracks of Uncle Horace Greeley on the *New York Tribune*.

In order to keep Ward in the neighborhood, Mark Twain tried to arrange for a lecture tour to include Aurora and Bodie. He hadn't seen life, Mark swore, until he had visited Esmeralda. But when Ward learned that the most recent celebrity to visit those diggings, a learned phrenologist who also gave recitations from Byron, had been shot by an unreconstructed horse thief in the middle of a stanza from "Childe Harold," he begged off.

Ward's departure happily coincided with the advent of 1864, and the combined farewell testimonial and New Year's celebration that resulted shook Virginia City right down to its bedplates. A delegation of miners presented the entertainer with a gold Albert watch chain so heavy that it sagged the pockets of his brocaded waistcoat. From Governor James Nye, an ardent admirer, came a citation naming Ward "Speaker of Pieces to the People of Washoe for the Term of his Natural Life." It was run up with a fancy border and a bewilderment of printer's ornaments on THE ENTERPRISE job press under Joe Goodman's special supervision.

Midafternoon of New Year's Day found the celebrants still seated at table or lying under it. The floor of the private room at Barnum's selected for the occasion was liberally encrusted with shattered champagne goblets, making it dangerous for a man to lie down, for Ward anticipated by three-quarters of a century A. A. Milne's sentiment:

> Like many of the upper class
> He loved the sound of smashing glass.

Empty champagne bottles by the score and other dead soldiers past counting formed a Boot Hill in the corner and bits of dismembered partridge and other viands illustrated the premises, for all the world as though Henry VIII and Cardinal Wolsey had been to supper. Waiters sagged wearily in corners and the flower of Washoe chivalry could be counted in rows of congress gaiters protruding from under the table.

True to the best traditions of THE TERRITORIAL ENTERPRISE, Mark Twain was on his feet, or nearly. He proposed a final toast to his close friend and bottle-scarred companion, "Artemus Ward, first in bars, first in pieces, first ——." But Ward was beyond caring and snored contentedly with his head on an empty jeroboam of Mumm's Extra, Specially Bottled for American Export. It had been a lovely party.

Climaxing the worldliness and association with names-that-made-news to which Mark Twain was becoming accustomed on the Comstock was the arrival of Adah Isaacs Menken for a stand at Maguire's Opera House in D Street in "Mazeppa," a garish melodrama full of heavy-handed rodomontade and production number scenes which delighted the miners of the West for a full theatrical generation.

Like her contemporary Lola Montez, The Menken loved life and lived it in a series of extravagances which appealed mightily even to such supposedly sophisticated figures of the great world as Dumas and Swinburne, and which simply bowled over the simple hearts of the Comstock's miners and millworkers at a time when Western chivalry was hard to separate from maudlin sentimentality over the nobility of womanhood.

The results of their infatuation with her performance of "Mazeppa" on the staff of The Territorial Enterprise, and the ensuing hard looks between Goodman and Maguire, have been elsewhere recounted in this volume. The riotous overtones of The Menken's stay other than on the stage in Virginia City became part of folklore.

The actress and her husband of the moment, a wretched little fop hilariously named Orpheus Kerr, held court in their apartments at the International Hotel. There she was serenaded at inappropriate hours by votive groups accompanied by military brass bands. Cases of champagne, even flowers, the ultimate Nevada extravagance then as now, were wafted to her suite by servitors themselves delighted to have a small part in the show of high life. M. L. Winn, proprietor of the International, remained on duty most of the hours of the twenty-four to see that his distinguished guest lacked no imaginable attention. The Menken received admirers swathed in canary-colored satin, lying before an open fire on a tiger skin, alternately sipping vintage cognac and eating French bonbons. Theda Bara, Nazimova, or any of the cinema queens of Hollywood's regal age might have taken lessons from her in the grand manner of a celebrity.

To be initiated into membership of the most exalted of all Comstock circles, she accepted from the hand of Tom Peasley, shortly to be murdered over a Carson City billiard table, the red belt of office in American Engine Company No. 2, on the balcony of the International. All accounts credit the first International—there were three of them—with a balcony, although only the conventional wooden awning over the sidewalk, of universal usage at the time, shows in contemporary lithographs of accepted veracity. To this, access could be had with only slight damage to dignity through a second-floor window and no doubt visiting notables accepted the homage of the crowd in this manner, but it surely was no balcony of state.

Confusion concerning the various International Hotels has addled the minds of many chroniclers. Even so meticulous a researcher as Effie Mona Mack makes the mistake of investing the first International, a two-story frame dwelling which was later removed intact to Austin, where it stands to this day, with an elevator, "the first west of Chicago." The first elevator west of Chicago was indeed in the International Hotel in Virginia City, competing for a photo finish with the sumptuous "rising rooms" of the Palace in San Francisco, but it was the third International Hotel, not the one known to Mark Twain.

The Menken was serenaded, wined, and dined throughout her stay on the Comstock. A street, now vanished, was named for her. So was a "Menken Shaft & Tunnel" mining company. She fought in the boxing ring with the superintendent of the Sierra Nevada, a local notable known as Joggles Wright, and floored him heavily, to the delight of everyone. At William Eckhoff's Sazarac Saloon, her portrait, painted by an itinerant artist in payment of a bar bill, occupied the place of honor above the back bar. The likeness, "naked to the pitiless storm," perished in the Great Fire of 1875 and today its place at the Sazarac is occupied by an equally unclad favorite of the Comstock 'sixties, Julia Bulette. The fair Julia of the twentieth century is naked to the pitiless gaze of a thousand tourists and as dead as a haddock, having just been murdered for her jewels by the scoundrelly John Millain.

In return for the signal favors accorded her in its columns, albeit they had been freighted with embarrassments, The Menken invited Mark Twain and Dan De Quille to Sunday evening dinner with her, as there was to be no performance that evening. Completing an intimate foursome was The Menken's traveling companion, Ada Clare, who wrote verses and enjoyed a reputation for having a liberal philosophy in matters of love. The miserable Orpheus wasn't asked and patrolled the hotel corridor, where he followed the arrival of a succession of waiters with envious gaze as they disappeared into the apartment that should have been his own. He wore a quilted smoking jacket and a red house cap with fringed tassel. Orpheus' wardrobe made a deep if not altogether favorable impression on the Comstock.

The affair was to be a gala supper party in the best Bohemian manner of Paris and San Francisco. Claret had been carefully brought to room temperature. Silver coolers of the best champagne were strategically placed around the table. There were quail in aspic, Strassburg *foie gras* on toast, larded filets of antelope, and "oysters, only two weeks from the shell, spiced, plump and *bueno*." The International's chef was in ecstasies. The apartment was furnished with rich Turkey carpets, costly draperies, rosewood chairs with crimson velvet cushions and fringes, and expensive marble-topped tables in the Italian style. The best of everything.

Alas, the feast of reason and flow of soul envisioned by the hostess was not to be. Conversation, which was to have been on an elevated plane, assumed a distinctly earthy turn and was concerned with mining matters. The Menken sought to return the occasion to its projected Olympian sphere with song. Mark Twain, who had been looking upon the Mumm's in the various coolers with admiration, was glad to oblige. His entire repertory consisted of a variation of "The Old Gray Mare," which he sang in a rich flat tenor. He knew only one stanza and, after repeating it eight or ten times, was prevailed upon to abandon the project.

The real trouble came in the form of dogs. The Menken troupe might have been mistaken for a dog and pony show from its animal life. Small Fidos and middle-size Towsers were underfoot wherever she went. There were French poodles clipped in ornate designs like flower beds in a formal garden and there were shaggy favorites who defied classification. The Menken loved them each and every one dearly and, as the party progressed, amused herself by feeding the zoo with loaf sugar soaked in cognac.

Ever imitative of the best in their owners and friends, the dogs were soon as drunk as Saturday night printers. One of them mistook Mark Twain's fashionable striped cashmere trousers for a canine convenience and the man of letters aimed a savage kick at the offender under the table.

There was a screech of mortal anguish as the Toast of Two Continents leaped from her chair "and rolled and groaned in agony" on a richly up-holstered sofa of French design. Clemens' sharp-pointed boot had caught The Menken squarely in her dainty shin, bruising it cruelly and causing the owner grief of an acute order. Arnica and towels iced in the handy wine buckets at length abated the pain and the actress protested loudly that all was forgiven.

But the party was over. Twain and De Quille excused themselves on pretended errands of professional urgency. They were needed at the office. A few minutes later found them in the bar of the William Tell House bending the ear of the bartender with the tale of their misfortunes.

The Menken departed for even greater triumphs in London, thoughtfully shedding Orpheus on the way, and Mark Twain never saw her again.

Mark Twain's own time in Nevada was running out.

Various occasions both personal and business absented Joe Goodman from the Lode with increasing frequency.

While the new quarters of THE ENTERPRISE were building in South C Street and machinery was being installed under the supervision of Denis Driscoll, with resulting confusion in and around the office, Goodman had taken off for a fortnight's relaxation at Lake Tahoe. There he purposed to get in some trout fishing and a little healthful drinking in the country.

Mark Twain assumed the duties of publisher in addition to those of city editor and in a short time found himself snowed under with responsibilities. Repeated pleas to return sent by daily post produced no results. Personal entreaties forwarded through the agency of the drivers of Allman & Co.'s Washoe and Virginia stages found no sympathetic ear. Goodman had a limitless supply of the best Monongahela and his Silver Doctors and Brown Hackles were decimating the ranks of the Sierra trout.

At length Clemens resorted to heroic measures.

One morning Goodman opened his edition of the day's ENTERPRISE and suddenly let out screams as though stabbed by a dozen assassins, followed by demands for his horse in Richard III accents.

Mark Twain had obviously gone insane or gotten crazy drunk the night before and the editorial page contained twenty references to prominent Nevadans that were criminally libelous per se, as well as personal allusions to the virtue of various good women of Virginia City, that would see THE ENTERPRISE run out of town and its proprietors lynched. Goodman's hair rose on his head as he galloped full tilt down the King's Canyon Highway toward a change of horses at Carson City.

Goodman arrived at THE ENTERPRISE office dusty and determined to have his editor's hide nailed to the door and that instanter. He found Mark Twain serenely occupied in a discussion of the relative merits of light and dark Lowenbrau with Mike McCluskey behind the bar at The Delta.

Apoplectically he demanded what had motivated Clemens to such thrice damned and inconceivable madness.

"What are you talking about?" Twain asked him, borrowing a copy of the day's ENTERPRISE from McCluskey. With trembling hands Goodman turned to the editorial columns to find them occupied in their entirety by an innocuous discussion of Lord Palmerston's most recent speech in the House of Commons. A single copy containing the infamous articles had been run off, the type hastily distributed, and the one copy sent up in Goodman's morning mail.

It brought him back to the office.

The next time Goodman went out of town, this time on business for the paper in San Francisco, Mark really got himself in hot water, and shortly thereafter was himself leaving Virginia City in a hack with drawn shutters.

The ladies of Carson City had recently given a charity ball of imposing proportions and social splendor to raise funds for the Sanitary Commission, predecessor of the Red Cross, which was performing valiantly among the wounded on the battlefronts of the East. They had triumphantly realized $3,000 but there was a trifling delay in forwarding it and Mark Twain thought the circumstances presented opportunities for a devastating hoax. He wrote a squib to the effect that it was rumored the money was to be diverted from its proper purpose and sent to a "miscegenation society somewhere in the East."

The Carson ladies, whose good intentions were greater than their sense of humor, replied in dignified accents that THE ENTERPRISE statement was a tissue of falsehoods and that its author was no gentleman.

A misunderstanding of a little kidding on the part of THE ENTERPRISE, nothing more, that could be corrected presently.

But the contretemps put ideas in the head of Editor James Laird of the *Virginia Daily Union*, then nursing a vendetta of Borgia dimensions against THE ENTERPRISE. Laird hastened to the support of the lady philanthropists with avenging adjectives. The author of THE ENTERPRISE slur on Nevada womanhood was a liar, a poltroon, and a puppy.

"Never before in a long period of newspaper intercourse," declared the *Union* warming to its theme, "never in any contact with a contemporary, however unprincipled he might have been, have we found an opponent, in statement or in discussion, who had no gentlemanly sense of professional propriety, who conveyed in every purpose of all his words such a grovelling disregard for truth, decency and courtesy as to seem to court the distinction of being understood as a vulgar liar."

The *Union*, in a word, called Mark Twain a practitioner of falsehood.

The Comstock roared with delight. This was the sort of thing the subscribers paid $16 a year for (fifty cents a month for delivery service). This was journalism in upper-case italics. THE ENTERPRISE and the *Union* were giving each other what for, and with gestures! The piles of papers on the counter at Dunlap & Drake, Periodicals, and at Bernhard Franz, "Latest Publications From the East, Stationary and Music," diminished as before a Washoe zephyr.

More delighted than anyone in town was Rollin Daggett, Mark Twain's overweight associate on the staff of THE ENTERPRISE. Clemens would be obliged to challenge Laird and there would be powder smoke and fun generally. Daggett and Steve Gillis represented to Mark that his sacred honor must clamor for avenging encounter. If, by mischance, he should get himself killed, they promised he should have a fine obituary notice in the best space THE ENTERPRISE afforded.

Clemens wasn't favorably impressed by their enthusiasm. He loathed the very idea of personal encounter and was a poor shot to boot. Besides, a happy thought, perhaps he was himself no gentleman and hence exempt from the chivalrous conduct expected of that estate. His family had been in trade.

Daggett and Gillis made short work of his protests. There was no College of Heralds on the Comstock. If Mark wasn't a gentleman he was surely a yeoman, a condition which permitted the bearing of arms, and as a member of THE ENTERPRISE staff he was bound to uphold the dignity of the paper. Hadn't Joe Goodman already done as much and hadn't Gillis himself faced no fewer than three adversaries under the terms of the code duello?

Mark Twain permitted himself to be launched into a lukewarm exchange of formal insults with Laird, in which the phrases "vile and slanderous communications," "unmitigated liar," "abject coward," "nothing to retract," and similar protestations of gentility and abhorrence of rascality predominated.

Finally, after a prolonged visit to Haynes' & Barry's Saloon and a couple of reassuring snorts at The El Dorado, Clemens uttered a masterpiece of defamation, proclaiming that Laird was not only an unmitigated liar and an abject coward but a liar on general principles. Also, snarled Mark Twain, Laird was a fool. This turned the trick.

Laird and Mark Twain, through their seconds, arranged to meet in a woodlot outside the city limits. Gillis and Daggett, the latter in the slouch black hat and talma of accepted convention for such office, acted as seconds for THE ENTERPRISE entrant. To test the Colt's Navy revolver which his principal would shortly carry, Gillis, an expert marksman with small arms, shot the head off a sage hen at the edge of the glade just as Laird's seconds arrived to make final arrangements.

Steve pressed the smoking gun into Mark Twain's hand and pounded the amazed editor on the back.

"That's good shooting, Sam," he cried jubilantly, "very good indeed, winging a bird in the air at thirty paces! You'll show old Laird a thing or two. But don't kill him; just blow his nasty face off!"

Laird's seconds clutched each other's sleeves and promised to return immediately. They had just time to get their man on the breakfast-time stage for Washoe City. It would have been murder to let him go up against such a marksman as the terrible-tempered Mark Twain! Flight was better than certain death!

But news of the proposed duel had come to the ear of authority and it so happened that it was authority whose head and ears Mark Twain had belabored with bladders. A warrant was issued for his arrest, but good-natured Governor Nye, a friend of THE ENTERPRISE, sent word that its service would be delayed by legal technicalities for twenty-four hours.

That night Mark Twain boarded the down stage for California and there was a vacant desk at THE TERRITORIAL ENTERPRISE.

Contemporary estimates of Mark Twain's two years on THE ENTERPRISE, uninfluenced by his later fame and success, are hard to come by. The bibliography of admiration, adulation, and reverence of the man is large and often emetic.

Joe Farnsworth, now the patriarch and grand old man at Carson City, where he was for years Nevada State Printer, was apprentice and later compositor and printer on THE ENTERPRISE in the early 'nineties and knew well and intimately many veterans of the paper's early years.

"From them I gathered the impression that Clemens was regarded as the prime s.o.b. of Virginia City when he was here," says Mr. Farnsworth. "He was personally unclean; his mind and conversation were foul and he was forever trying to insinuate double meanings into his copy which had to be scrupulously read on the desk before it could go to the printer. He was notoriously a drink cadger and mean as catsmeat when it came to setting them up on the bar. One old fellow who knew him well used a phrase I remember: 'Mark Twain had no ear muffs on when somebody else was buying. He could hear a live one order a round three doors from where he was standing, but he was deaf as a post when his turn came to shout.'

"The mean practical jokes that were arranged at Mark Twain's expense were not hilariously good-natured gags. They were evidence that his associates thoroughly disliked him. A great deal of hogwash has been written in admiration of the man as a writer, but I never heard any admiration expressed for him personally by men who knew him personally. The news that rumors of his death had been exaggerated was unpleasant news everywhere in Virginia City."

"Athens of The Coast"

F THE number of papers published in a city is looked upon as a reflex of the intelligence and enterprise of its inhabitants, then Virginia has the right to claim for itself the title of the 'Athens' of the Pacific Coast."

So read the introductory paragraphs devoted to newspapers in Charles Collins' "Mercantile Guide and Directory For Virginia City, Gold Hill, Silver City and American City for 1864–65."

"The Enterprise is particularly favored by mining Secretaries as a medium for advertising their assessment sales," says Collins further on. "'Mark Twain' and 'Dan De Quille' occupy a local and corresponding prominence in its columns."

The reading notice is generous since, although it had advertised in the "Virginia Directory" the year before, The Enterprise was not this year represented in the classified section, then, as in today's phone books, printed on yellow pages. A tiff between Collins and Joe Goodman may have arisen over the printing of the directory in San Francisco instead of at The Enterprise job plant.

Athens of the Pacific Coast or not, Virginia City was becoming famous for its newspaper and their fame was to be mutually interdependent for several decades to come.

The brief interlude of Mark Twain's association with The Territorial Enterprise were the years of the newspaper's wild oats. They witnessed the wild and untrammeled flowering of the Comstock's bonanzas and their first rigadoon of riches on the sunswept slopes of Mount Davidson, of Virginia City's first taste of abundant wealth with the promise of incalculable riches to come, and they also witnessed Washoe's first descent into borrasca, its first of several serious conflagrations, and the breaking on its stony headlands of the greatest crime wave it was to know in its long history of violence.

Sam Clemens was the symbol of The Enterprise' heady youth and brilliant promise. Its more prudently ordered maturity commenced almost as Mark Twain departed and was represented by the more considered

84

judgment of Dan De Quille, whose destinies were linked with those of the paper, not briefly and audaciously like Mark Twain's, but over more than three decades of sustained brilliance and professional success.

Editors whose names lived but briefly on the paper's masthead came and went, some of them to golden destinies elsewhere in the ever growing frontier West. During the short period when the paper was published in North C Street from a loft over Joe Barnert's clothing store and next door to its old neighbor in C Street, Wells Fargo, Goodman had hired as assistant editor George Francis Daw and, following him, Captain Joe Plunkett. Later, the seat at the head of conference table was occupied by George W. Lyon, afterward editor in chief of the *Seattle Daily Times*, who in turn was succeeded by Thomas H. Gardiner, a Sacramento journalist of some contemporary note.

The paper's first business manager on the Comstock was William H. Barstow, who was followed by Henry P. Cohen. "In journalism almost anybody can run the brain box of a paper," wrote Sam Davis of Cohen some years later, "but it takes the smartest man in the establishment to run the cash box and keep the creditors of the sheet paid up."

Cohen must have been versatile indeed and the fact is attested by the circumstance that, not only did the financial affairs of THE ENTERPRISE soar under his careful management, but after Mark Twain left he was asked by Goodman to take over the post of dramatic critic for the paper.

In 1863, while Samuel L. Clemens was still listed on Page 183 of the *Nevada Directory* as "local editor, THE TERRITORIAL ENTERPRISE," Goodman and McCarthy had sold a small share in the property to Denis Driscoll, an old-time printer from San Francisco in the days of Sam Brannan's *Star* and the *Golden Era*, when that breezy paper had been the official posting board for challenges to duels and where he had first met Joe Goodman.

Driscoll seems to have been something of a pioneer in the mechanics of newspaper production, for it was shortly after his buying of a share in the property that THE ENTERPRISE purchased a lot on the east side of South C Street and installed the first steam-activated press in Nevada. It is still published from those premises.

A fine, two-story red-brick building, gorgeous with the trim and gingerbread dear to the heart of architect and businessman alike in Victorian times, was erected. It had the conventional wooden awning over the sidewalk, surrounded by a stout balustrade which provided a fine vantage point for viewing the parades and civic receptions of which the Comstock never tired. The awning, too, is there to this day.

85

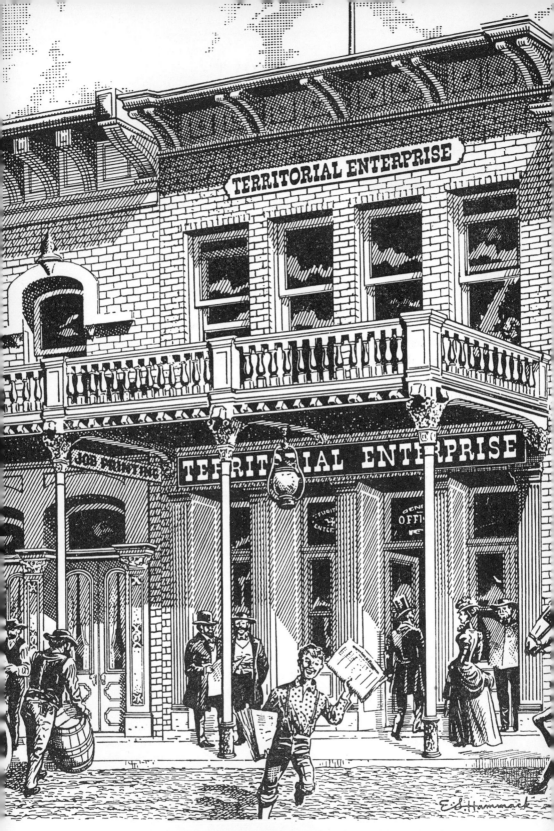

TWO-STORY BRICK building into which The Enterprise moved in 1863 and from which it is still published, as it looked in the 'sixties.

The advent of the steam press was the occasion for another of the many days marked with a star in Virginia City history. The machine came up from San Francisco in sections loaded aboard vast wains powered by oxen and piloted by the most profane race of men in all the Western strain. Its progress through Placerville, as Hangtown was now called, to Sportsman's Hall and eventually Strawberry, named not for a fruit but for a flagrantly mean innkeeper named Berry who fed travelers' horses on straw instead of hay, was daily reported to the Comstock.

In due time it arrived and winches and cranes from the mines were used to ease its components into the basement, where they crouched in the gloom, as Gene Fowler says, "like spavined dinosaurs."

Came the great night for the first run of the paper in steam.

Compositors and editors had planned to assemble their copy and have it on the imposing stones early as a special safeguard against any delay that might arise from unfamiliar facilities in the press room, but the management had reckoned without the Comstock's saloonkeepers. Promptly at midnight, the crucial hour in the production of the morrow's paper, when twenty compositors at their cases were working against a tight schedule, there appeared a parade of men in white aprons bearing gifts.

Every saloonkeeper and hotelier in Virginia City had sent in a trifling token of good will and esteem ranging from magnums of the best French champagne to growlers of Pilsener, decanters of the dew of Bourbon County and the Steamboat gin that was a favored tipple of compositors.

From that moment Driscoll's carefully rehearsed production schedule began coming apart at the seams. Whole galleys of nonpareil appeared in proof to be in a state of illegible confusion. Advertising matter of an urgent nature was conveyed to imposing stones by palsied hands and landed on the floor in shocking pi. Somebody dropped a bottle squarely among the innards of the fine new press and time was taken out to remove the shards. The printers themselves were unfamiliar with the machinery and short snorts from bottles of Steamboat did nothing to increase their efficiency. Co-ordination between editorial and mechanical departments approached zero as a limit. THE TERRITORIAL ENTERPRISE was the official organ of bedlam.

The net result was a paper eight hours late on the street, whose typographical infamies set the meticulous Driscoll to toying with thoughts of suicide. Actually, in a day before out-of-town mail deadlines and paper train schedules had to be met, a late paper was nothing very serious. Local subscribers took it in their stride and Goodman good-naturedly forgave all. Mark Twain, however, departed from THE ENTERPRISE offices in bad order and slept in a C Street doorway until a constable discovered him and helped him up Union Street in the direction of home. Mark sent a note to the office next day to say that "a severe quinsy had settled on his mind" and didn't appear at his desk for three days.

The stirring events in the East that came to a climax in the concluding days of the Civil War had their stirring counterparts in Nevada. Led by Virginia City's Father of Mining Law, William Stewart, the voters of the territory had set in motion the machinery to make Nevada a state. The movement had had the fullest support of Joe Goodman and THE ENTERPRISE, which, as an additional argument to throwing Nevada's weight and wealth behind the Union cause, never tired of repeating that statehood would relieve the commonwealth of the almost unbearable corruption and greed of territorial courts.

The ermine of Washoe justice had become moth-eaten in the course of early mining litigation, when every judge had his price and was only considered dishonest if he sold out to both parties to a suit. Despite all the opposition which could be devised by Chief Justice George Turner, Stewart secured the necessary signatures to a petition for the resignation of the whole Supreme Court of Nevada, and THE TERRITORIAL ENTERPRISE published it in its entirety.

At the territorial election that fall, Nevadans voted by a majority of 9,000 to take advantage of the complex constitutional machinery permitting them to become the thirty-sixth state, and on October 31, 1864, Governor Nye received word from Washington which enabled him to wire Joe Goodman from Carson City: "Nevada is this day admitted to the Union. The pain is over. The child is born. Let us see to it that Nevada is not only in the Union but for the Union." Goodman was able to have an ENTERPRISE extra edition on the streets of Virginia City the same day that President Lincoln had signed the act of admission, no mean achievement over a distance of nearly 3,000 miles and in the face of the imperfections of the existing telegraph lines.

The news of Lee's surrender in the spring of the following year was the occasion for the most thunderous debauch in the history of the Old West. THE ENTERPRISE was able only to get an outline of the dispatch, a simple statement of fact devoid of all detail, on a bulletin hung from the front of its building, before its staff from owner to the least apprentice was dissolved in the universal sea of whisky. All business save that of saloons on the Comstock suspended and for two days the very notion of attempting to get out a printed edition was considered hilarious.

No newspaper of any sort appeared in Virginia City, Gold Hill, or Silver City. No editor could have prepared the copy, no compositor could have set it, and no printer could have activated a press. And, as somebody reasonably enough remarked, had there been a paper available nobody would have been able to read it.

At the end of three days, when the stock of whisky on the Comstock was exhausted and the fallen lay three deep in the gutters of C Street, THE ENTERPRISE and the *Union* pooled their resources of ague and katzenjammer to produce a four-page extra with the news of Appomattox for the first time in the printed record.

Close on the joyful tidings came the mournful intelligence of Lincoln's death. ENTERPRISE extras which issued from the presses with the arrival of each of a melancholy succession of telegrams were torn to pieces, before they could be read, by frantic crowds which pressed around the paper's building in C Street, in such numbers as actually to imperil its stoutly built awning held up by substantial cast iron pillars. The news came over the wires in short takes and was crammed into the forms by printers as soon as they arrived.

First Dispatch:

His Excellency President Lincoln was assassinated at the theater tonight.

Second Dispatch:

President Lincoln died at 8:30 this morning and Secretary Stewart a few minutes past 9.

Third Dispatch:

Reports are contradictory. It is reported that President died at 7:22.

Then the Western Union wires went dead. Rioting had broken out in San Francisco, where mobs were destroying the premises of newspapers suspected of Secessionist sympathies. Troops had been called from the Presidio and martial law proclaimed. Somehow, in the excitement which gripped the city the telegraph wires had been cut and Washoe heard no more for twenty-four hours.

It was enough for Virginia City, however, that Lincoln was dead. Memorial services that afternoon filled Maguire's Opera to capacity to hear Bishop O. W. Whitaker of St. Paul's Episcopal Church read the Litany and services for the dead. In the street outside thousands wept unabashedly as his voice came through the open doors of the auditorium: "I am the Resurrection and the Light, whoso believest——"

Then Joe Goodman, friend of Lincoln and of the Union, publisher of THE TERRITORIAL ENTERPRISE, first citizen of the Comstock, read a tribute to the glorious dead:

> A nation lay at rest. The mighty storm
> That threatened their good ship with direful harm
> Had spent its fury, and the tired and worn
> Sank in sweet slumber, as the springtime morn
> Dawned with a promise that the strife should cease
> And war's grim face smiled in a dream of peace. . . .

Next to Mark Twain more has been written about Dan De Quille than any other member of THE ENTERPRISE staff in its early days. The emphasis should have been reversed for, during his Nevada years and regardless of later achievements, Clemens was in every way De Quille's inferior either as man of the world or newspaperman.

Much of Mark Twain's talent was purely and simply acquisitive, his originality often open to suspicion, and whatever good product was evolved out of his Comstock experience reflected the maturity, good judgment, and worldly wisdom of his associates, Goodman, Steve Gillis, and Dan De Quille.

As was the case almost without exception with Western newspapermen at the time and, happily, later, De Quille was a master hand with a bottle. All-night sessions at Barnum's or the International seemingly left him without scar, and hard-rock miners and horny-handed enginemen learned to respect his almost bottomless capacity.

De Quille's partiality to the "east wind from the brewery" did not always extend to universal tolerance, however. One night he and Steve Gillis were knocking them off with the regularity of an Eddy clock at the Fredericksburg Brewery Saloon when De Quille was moved to sentimental apostrophe of his little daughter back in Iowa. Her virtues and excellences were recalled in glowing tribute, for when in wine De Quille was more than commonly eloquent.

Moved by De Quille's infatuated periods, Gillis leaned across the cigar butts and overset glasses and said: "Dan, that's just the sort of girl I've been looking for. Send for her to come out and I'll marry her."

De Quille's face darkened with rage and, with a tumbler of Old Noble Treble Crown arrested in mid-air, he thundered: "No son of a bitch who drinks whisky can ever look at my little girl."

The matrimonial project was shelved.

"ATHENS OF THE COAST"

THE ENTERPRISE, with De Quille as its mining editor and authority on precious metals, succeeded the *Sacramento Union* as the universal reporter of the California and Nevada diggings. The coverage of the *Union* had been definitive, but the accuracy of De Quille's forecasts, his profound knowledge of the Lode in its every detail, and his unassailable probity gave THE ENTERPRISE a weight, authority, and prestige enjoyed by no other newspaper of the frontier.

Few newspapers had so much local color to draw on; none but THE ENTERPRISE had De Quille. Even such cynical participants in the recurrent frauds and swindles implicit in mining speculation as Slippery Jim Fair acknowledged De Quille's scrupulous honesty and complete unavailability to purchase. Privy as he repeatedly was to secrets of the bonanzas which, had he chosen to profit by them, would have made him wealthy, Dan remained a poor man all his life, never living beyond the $50 weekly salary paid him by THE ENTERPRISE for thirty-one years, and the much smaller fees for correspondence sent to San Francisco papers. When the tenth edition of the *Encyclopædia Britannica* paid him an honorarium of six pounds for an article on Nevada, the sum was much more than a token to Dan and he set up drinks for all comers at The Delta in recognition of the windfall.

De Quille's complete inaccessibility to influence of any sort shines the brighter in comparison to many and many a mining, financial, and stock market editor of his generation whose columns were notoriously available to the promotion of dubious or even nonextant properties. Nevada's peerless senators, John Percival Jones and William Morris Stewart, once participated in a promotion scheme for a Utah mine up Little Cottonwood Canyon which had international repercussions. The Little Emma, hilariously named for one of Brigham Young's wives, was salted and valueless to a degree that aroused unusual admiration in Montgomery Street, and the owners sold several million dollars' worth of its stock to unsuspecting investors in England. To accomplish this superswindle they lined the pocket of the financial editor of the august and presumably impervious London *Times*, and in the ensuing scandal the American minister to the Court of St. James's was recalled and Anglo-American amity achieved an all-time low.

But though the Thunderer might be bribed, no taint of suspicion ever attached to the mining editor of THE TERRITORIAL ENTERPRISE. To control its columns it was necessary to purchase the property in its entirety, which eventually happened.

Indicative of De Quille's reputation for careful reporting and utter incorruptibility was the circumstance that when it came time for the bonanza firm of Flood, Fair, Mackay, and O'Brien to announce the stupendous ore bodies in Con-Virginia, ever afterward known as The Big Bonanza, they selected THE TERRITORIAL ENTERPRISE to have the story exclusively and De Quille, as its mining editor, to have the beat.

De Quille published his own estimate of the ore bodies in what was the most important and exciting story ever carried in the paper. He announced that to his belief there was $116,748,000 in "the finest chloride ore filled with streaks and bunches of the richest black silver sulphurettes" actually in sight in the great stope of the Con-Virginia. This sum was but half what De Quille privately estimated in his own mind. The implication was that in the California mine adjacent to it and also owned by the bonanza firm there might be comparable or even greater wealth.

The story swept around the world. The value of the two mines on the San Francisco exchange rose so rapidly transactions could not be recorded, from $40,000,000 to a dazzling $160,000,000. They carried other Comstock properties with them to dizzying heights. De Quille's estimate was doubled a few days later and characterized as the most conservative understatement by the director of the mint at Carson City. Other experts went to even greater lengths, but in the end De Quille's estimate proved the most accurate of all.

The effect of these excitements was almost incalculable. Foreign exchanges fluctuated violently on the bourses and stock markets of the entire world. Bismarck ordered Germany off the silver standard. Fantastic fortunes were made by speculators and the Comstock's future potentialities estimated in astronomical figures.

Through it all De Quille remained content with his regular salary on THE ENTERPRISE' books. He had chronicled and participated at firsthand in events that made archmillionaires by the score and never profited from his inside knowledge.

"No man could corrupt Dan De Quille," wrote Judge Goodwin years afterward. "No man could scare him. . . . His resourcefulness in a newspaper office was wonderful, his industry untiring and his brain exhaustless."

Joe Farnsworth was apprentice in THE ENTERPRISE composing room when De Quille still lived in A Street as an emeritus of the staff and often spent the evening with him, hearing tales of the heroic youth of the Comstock.

"Everyone on the staff hated Mark Twain," Farnsworth recalled, "and everyone really loved De Quille. I think he was the most wonderful old man I ever knew. He couldn't say three words to you before you were his friend for life and wanted to put your arms around him.

"At the time I speak of he was poor as a church mouse. I don't know what he did with his money, but in his old age I know he didn't drink at all. His beard, which had never been anything but thin, was reduced to about three straggling hairs and he wore an old slouch hat and a short cloak of the sort known as a talma and which even then was long out of date.

"He was the grand old man of Virginia City and everyone in Nevada knew him by sight. I never knew a man more loved and respected."

In keeping with his gentle nature and reluctance to harm the feelings of anyone, De Quille's hoaxes—quaints, he liked to call them—had none of the aspect of personal malice which characterized the imitative stories of Mark Twain. They were meticulously devised and so altogether preposterous as to rank as masterpieces of American folklore.

Most celebrated of them was, of course, "The Mystery of the Savage Sump," which pretended to scientific proof that a subterranean river from the abyss of Lake Tahoe flowed through the underground workings of Virginia City, flooding the mines, and was prepared with such narrative skill and plausibility that almost a hundred years after it was written readers first encountering it and not warned in advance of its nature are gulled into believing it to be established fact.

In the vein of twentieth-century pseudo-science fiction Dan then invented a suit of solar armor for the protection from the sun of prospectors in the Nevada desert. This useful invention was a rubber suit similar to a diver's with an early, deep-freeze device cunningly built in. One afternoon the inventor started across Death Valley in a temperature of 117 degrees to demonstrate his patent. He never arrived at his destination and his body was found by searchers some days later, frozen to death in a sitting position with an icicle pendent from its nose. The machine had got out of hand and killed its inventor.

All Nevada held its breath to see who might be conned into swallowing this whopper and the eventual sucker exceeded the wildest expectations. The erudite scientific editor of the London *Times* (evidently the paper had learned nothing of Nevada duplicity from the affair of the Little Emma) devoted a solemn three columns to advocating the adoption of De Quille's invention for British armies in the tropics.

If the thunders of THE ENTERPRISE could be turned against the mighty for their undoing, there were also times when its editors sought more vulnerable targets. The paper's own private version of the man-eating shark, which, by journalistic proverb, is the only altogether safe object for denunciation, was the camels of the Comstock. These derelict animals had been imported by the Federal government some years before and, found unsuited to Army use, had been sold to private operators in the desert transport of Nevada and Arizona. For a time they had been employed in the salt trade between Austin and Eureka and Virginia City, but had been at length turned loose to shift for themselves, to haunt the midnight wastelands like Flying Dutchmen of the desert. Horses and other animals were terrified of them and they were prevented by municipal regulation from the streets of Virginia City by daylight.

An itinerant printer, newly employed on THE ENTERPRISE, had spent his first night in Virginia City looking upon the wine in the Great Republic Saloon in Taylor Street and next morning confronted the foreman with the demand to cash in his string. He complained that the brand of whisky sold in Virginia City caused him to see things at night, camels to be precise, and that he was leaving town right now. Next thing he knew he'd be having imaginary ants and he wanted out.

The foreman good-naturedly told him that in all probability he had indeed seen actual flesh-and-blood camels and had nothing to worry about.

"I want my money now, twice as urgently," screamed the man of rules and spaces. "I don't work for any goddam print shop where the foreman sees camels, too!"

In May 1869 THE ENTERPRISE had at the homeless camels editorially, under the heading "The Camel Nuisance."

The camels have made their reappearance on the Carson River, more numerous than ever, and again the lives and limbs of the traveling public along that route are to be endangered. Well may our citizens cry aloud at this nuisance. "How long, O Lord, how long!" We beg to call the attention of the Grand Jury of Lyon County to these camels, or rather the owners of them, and suggest that they be presented at the next session as public, crying nuisances, and recommend such measures as will protect the people riding and driving from loss of life or accidents. Unfortunately, we have no idea that this will be done, but as conservators of the public weal, we conceive it to be a part of our duty to call attention to this camel danger. It was only last fall, during the Presidential campaign that we had occasion to record the narrow escape of two very prominent citizens of this city, their team taking fright at the sight of the camels on the road, as is usually the case whenever they are seen by horses and mules, the danger being greater with the latter, but we fear nothing will be done until somebody is cut and injured, and then probably the most stringent measures will be adopted to cure the evil, when just now a little prevention is needed to be equally effective, to say nothing of the gain to the party who may from present neglect be ultimately injured.

At another time at about this period THE ENTERPRISE carried the following delightful picture of a first citizen of the Lode who had tarried too long among the beakers at the Concordia or Ward & Heffron's Argentine Saloon in South C Street.

RAMBLES OF A "SPECKLED BIRD"

(July 9, 1868)

The night of the late "glorious Fourth" we bent our weary and virtuous footsteps homeward just at that hour when no sheeted dead but the "three sheeted" living are aboard. We came to the stairs at the corner of C and Taylor streets, and were about ascending, on our way to B street, when we saw before us, some half a dozen steps up the stairs in the deep shadow of the California Bank (an institution that often does cast a very black shadow, as many who have been under it can testify), the figure of a man.

He was seated, and resting his head and right shoulder against the wall of the building, in whose shadow he was reposing. His black slouched hat was pushed from the exact apex of his head by its contact with the rail, and rested in a style of graceful bravado over his left ear. We felt that we stood in the presence of some ardent but inconsiderate patriot, and thus saluted the recumbent figure: "What, ho! stranger, why halt you here?" The head of the figure was slowly raised and turned toward us; the slouched hat was pushed back, and we saw the dim outlines of a face standing out from a mop of disordered hair. We could distinguish no single feature in the darkness, yet we felt that a pair of inflamed eyes were staring stupidly at us.

"Who are you, old fellow?" asked we, "and what is the matter with you?"

Slowly the head turned toward us, and a voice that we with some difficulty recognized as that of Gideon Groanwell, one of the pillars of the church, a powerful exhorter and a mighty disburser of psalmody before the Lord said: "I'm the speckled bird of the mountains of Gilboa; stay me with flagons, comfort me with apples, for I am sick of love."

"Bah!" cried we, "get up and go home; why, you are tight as a brick!"

"Home? no, sir—no sir! Live while you live; life is short, sir; we are flowers of the field, sir, like lilies of er valley—lilies of the valley. Let us not be proud or puffed up, sir; for we are all lilies of er valley. I'm not puffed up sir,—nozur. I've been among the daughters of the Teutons, sir; even among the cunning dancers whose feet are beautiful on the mountains—whose white feet twinkle as alabaster in the waters of the Jordan—also have I been among the sons of Jubal, even such as handle the harp, the organ and the psaltery. I have danced even as David danced and drank wine even as Noah when he

95

began to be a husbandman, sir; but tell it not in Gath, publish it not in the columns of The Enterprise! I've looked on the faces of the Philistines, even as Samson looked on the face of Delilah—now, sir, I'm ready to carry off er gates of Gaza." Springing to his feet he cried: "The gates of Gaza, sir, show me the gates of Gaza; I'm on it!"

We now felt it our duty to speak quite plainly to Gideon of the impropriety of a man of his standing becoming clamorous to tackle the gates of Gaza at such an hour of the night and hinted that the doors of the station-house would be the first hinged obstacle he would be likely to encounter, and a policeman his first Philistine—"sons of Belial" he pronounced them. At once he soon was changed.

"Woe is me," cried he, "how could I dare to burn incense unto gods! silver spread into plates is brought from Tarshish and gold from Uphaz, who shall be able to keep shekels of silver or wedges of gold, or rings of jasper, or sardonyx, or topaz, or jacinth, or beryl, or chrysolites, or amethist from these greedy Delilahs—Delilahs who are not appeased with hair, whose hands a whole wig would not stay! for the mountains I will take up a weeping and wailing and for er habitations of er wilderness lamendation! I'm the speckled bird from the cellars and from the secret places of the daughters of the Teuton—I flee from them; they are black as the tents of Kedar! Tell it not in Gath, sir, publish it not in the streets of Reno, neither in the pages of the *Mazepper*! How can I face that good woman, Hanner?—bone of my bones and flesh of my flesh—for in the day that I see her face will there come, that self-same day, a blowing of trumpets, a breaking of seals and a pouring out of vials! No, sir! Don't talk to me, sir, or wrestle with Jacob at the ford of Jabbok; whither thou goest I cannot go; whither thou lodgest I cannot lodge! I'm er speckled bird of er mountains of Gilboa, sir, and thither I flee to lift up my voice against the woman in scarlet, sir, even the daughter of Teuton, like a hungry pelican in the wilderness, sir!"

With these words the "speckled bird" spread its wings and took its unsteady and zig zag flight, and doubtless soon had some of its fine feathers plucked out by the good Hannah, that mighty blower of trumpets, breaker of seals and outpourer of vials before the Lord.

Goodman's final adieu to the newspaper he had made rich, famous, and influential was, in a manner of speaking, his greatest as well as ultimate triumph.

In 1872 William Sharon had been candidate for United States Senator and Goodman, who despised him heartily, had printed, on the occasion of the candidate's return from a trip to San Francisco, a welcoming editorial.

Your unexpected return, Mr. Sharon, has afforded no opportunity for public preparation, and you will consequently accept these simple remarks as an unworthy but earnest expression of the sentiments of a people who feel that they would be lacking in duty and self-respect if they failed upon such an occasion to make a deserved recognition of your acts and character. You are probably aware that you have returned to a community where you are feared, hated and despised . . . Your career in Nevada for the past nine years has been one of merciless rapacity. You fastened yourself upon the vitals of the State like a hyena, and woe to him who disputed with you a single coveted morsel of your prey . . . You cast honor, honesty and the commonest civilities aside. You broke faith with men whenever you could subserve your purpose by doing so. . . .

With few exceptions, Nevadans—most of whom the astute and cold-blooded manager for the gelid Bank of California had somehow managed to cheat, rob, or antagonize—cheered deafeningly for THE TERRITORIAL ENTERPRISE. That Sharon had unquestionably done the bidding of his principals in most of the swindles engineered by "the Bank crowd" was generally acknowledged, but Sharon combined an aloof personality with a degree of aristocratic reticence poorly suited to the hearty ways and manner of the Nevada frontier and his comeuppance would probably have been cheered even had his conduct been characterized by more moral rectitude than it was.

Sharon failed of election to the Senate and retired to the Montgomery Street private office of Darius Ogden Mills to lick his wounds. They were indeed grievous and required the most expensive sort of treatment.

A realist who frankly acknowledged that he could never achieve the toga so long as the destinies of THE ENTERPRISE were under the control of the terrible-tempered Goodman, Sharon and the Bank of California raised a mighty war chest to assure his election in the voting of 1874. For a sum today unknown but obviously of impressive dimensions, they purchased THE TERRITORIAL ENTERPRISE, lock, stock, and paper cutter, and reorganized it as the Enterprise Publishing Company with stock equally divided between the Virginia & Truckee Railroad—whose Superintendent, Henry Yerington, was a whiskered serf of the bank—and other holding companies of the Mills organization.

With Daggett as editor, THE ENTERPRISE' estimate of Sharon revised its casting of him as the Comstock Cataline and took a more cheerful view of his activities.

Mr. Sharon has lived in Nevada for ten years [so said the reformed ENTERPRISE] and by his sagacity, energy and nerve, he has amassed a fortune. This is his crime. He has done what he has done without once breaking his plighted word, without once violating one principle of business honor. While he was doing this he has carried, with his own, the fortunes of hundreds, and has never once betrayed a trust or confidence. . . . The present prosperity of Western Nevada is more due to him than to any other ten men, and could his work here be stricken out, with it would go at once two thirds of our people, improvements and wealth.

With the support of THE TERRITORIAL ENTERPRISE instead of its opposition, Sharon promptly achieved his ambition to be United States Senator from Nevada. In addition to the price of the newspaper it was generally understood that he had spent another quarter million purchasing the suffrage of the enlightened electorate. According to the standards of the time, however, it was an honest election. Every man got paid for his vote, didn't he?

The true amateur of the folklore of the old American West must eventually, and without alternative, become a connoisseur also of combustion, a collector of conflagrations, a retrospective buff and student of holocausts. For, along with its other qualities and characteristics, the West of the nineteenth century, and indeed well on into the twentieth, was one of the most inflammable locales of which history has any record. Fire was as much a vital hazard as gunfire, and gunfire was practically universal.

By design or by mischance, the greatest cities of the East, New York, Boston, Atlanta, and Chicago, were all reduced to ashes at some time during the period between 1835 and 1875, and the habit of conflagration came to the West with the pioneers. It came around the Horn with the Argonauts, so that San Francisco was burned as flat as a collapsed opera hat four separate times during the years 1849 and 1850, and the most terrible conflagration to date—a bigger one was in store some years later—in 1851 reduced to ashes seven million dollars' worth of real estate, and the city came the nearest it ever has come to discouragement in the matter of rebuilding.

The Gold Rush carried destruction by fire with it to the boom camps of the Mother Lode, so that Columbia and Grass Valley, as well as numerous less notable communities, were burned out, some more than once. As a state, however, it is doubtful if even California burned with such fearful and continued incandescence as did Nevada. During its booming years, hardly a mining camp or established city of importance but was destroyed at least once, some of them repeatedly, by disastrous conflagrations. Pioche, Eureka, Rawhide, Hamilton, and, last of all, Goldfield, went up in expensive smoke, while, just across the California line, Bodie, wickedest and most notorious of all pioneer camps, and Greenwater, high above Death Valley, became for a brief moment torches in the desert.

So inflammable were the mining camps of the Mother Lode that, throughout the Gold Rush decades, the destruction of an entire diggings, with its tent and shack residences and false-front saloons, was regarded with equanimity by the inhabitants, who lived an al fresco existence until the town should rise again from the ashes. Water was scarce, fire engines of primitive design, and, as often as not, the engine house and its gooseneck pumper were leveled before the volunteers could arrive on the scene.

Inevitably the newspapers of the frontier suffered in these recurrent holocausts. During the Great Fire at Eureka, the staff of the *Sentinel* assembled at the sound of the tocsin and were able to get an extra on the street just before the roof fell in about their ears. When Greenwater met its doom, valiant attempts were made to save the edifice of the *Greenwater Chuckwalla* with bottled beer from Metzger's Saloon, next door, there being no water handy. But in vain.

During the recurrent fires which swept Virginia City's tents and shacks in the early years, THE ENTERPRISE never had been forced to suspend publication. True, on one occasion its precarious quarters in A Street, not fifty feet from where this story is being written, were burned out, but so modest were its mechanical resources at the time that the staff was able to carry type cases, imposing stone, and Ramage press into the street, where the paper was composed and printed with the story of its own misfortune.

In October 1875 the affairs of the Comstock were at their fullest flower. A thousand stamp mills were dancing an eccentric rigadoon of riches on the side of Sun Mountain. A population of 25,000, one third of it underground in the mines at any hour of day or night, kept its saloons jammed with the thirsty, its bagnios working overtime, its places of public assembly in ferment. Stock in Consolidated Virginia, which had sold for $100 a share not so long ago, was bringing $5,000. Flood, Fair, Mackay, and O'Brien, the silver kings of the Comstock, were indulging a taste for mansions in San Francisco, stock farms in California, private cars over their own railroad lines, titled sons-in-law, and the presentation of their wives and daughters at the Court of St. James's.

It was at this time that a delivery boy, who brought the morning edition of THE ENTERPRISE to the doorstep of a lodginghouse at the south end of B Street, smelled smoke and saw flames dancing along the ridgepole. Within the hour, the Cosmopolis of the West was engulfed in flames. In some precincts, the approach of doom was so swift that the fine new Amoskeag steam fire engines, which were just coming into vogue, were destroyed in the firehouses. False fronts came down into C Street with terrifying clatter. Gone to glory was the beautiful Church of St. Mary's-in-the-Mountains, sent aloft in a blast of giant powder in an attempt to save the shaft head of the Con-Virginia and California mines. The premises of Roos Brothers, the stylish, present-day San Francisco clothiers, erupted in a fountain of flaming gents' suits, opera hats, and Inverness capes. Wells Fargo's express offices went up in a tower of flame visible at Austin, on the Reese River, 175 miles to the east. The International Hotel went to glory, along with 2,000 dwellings and $10,000,000 worth of assorted real estate. So did THE TERRITORIAL ENTERPRISE.

Some of its properties were driven wildly to safety on the outskirts of the doomed town; but its priceless files—the record of the dancing years of the Old West, the repository of much glory, pathos, and delight—were lost. Gone were the editions dripping with the blood of the Piute war, gone were the dispatches which had lifted the hearts of the miners with the news of Appomattox. No known copy exists telling of the first assay which brought half the world streaming to Washoe with the promise of silver. No living eye has seen THE ENTERPRISE account of the murder of Julia Bulette, Virginia City's queen of the strumpets and darling of the fire companies. An era of the West ended with the Great Fire of Virginia City, and much of the record of the era itself was lost.

When the Day Book of THE ENTERPRISE resumed a few weeks later, a new hand wrote in the neat Spencerian entries and tall columns of figures. Whatever clerk, with goose quill and pounce, had kept the books until then never resumed. Perhaps he had had enough of a city which could, almost in its entirety, go up in smoke in three hours. Perhaps he perished.

Managing editor of THE ENTERPRISE at the time of the fire was George Daly, whose son Alex Daly, almost three-quarters of a century after the event, remembered watching the conflagration from a vantage point on the slopes of Mount Davidson. As the flames swept down C Street, fanned by a fatal "zephyr," the elder Daly, according to his son, foresaw the possibility of printing next day's paper elsewhere and passed a number of forms in which was locked the type for the last edition through the cellar window and himself had to be evacuated by the same route when the upper stories were in flames.

Alex Daly also recalled that part of the next day's ENTERPRISE was printed on butcher's stock because of a shortage of conventional newsprint in the storerooms of the *Gold Hill News*. If such was indeed the case, no example of this improvisation has survived nor did the front-page logotype of THE ENTERPRISE everyone knew appear in the paper for October 28. It seems probable that despite their salvage through the window the type and furniture of THE ENTERPRISE were not, for mechanical reasons, available to use on the press of the *News*.

George Daly left THE ENTERPRISE shortly thereafter to follow a career of geologist appraising mining prospects throughout the West, and was killed by Apaches while investigating new diggings near Deming, New Mexico, in 1881.

Virginia City's Great Fire occurred on the morning of October 26 and no extant file shows a paper for October 27, so it may be presumed that on that day it missed an issue.

On October 28, however, THE TERRITORIAL ENTERPRISE once more appeared, with only two pages and with a masthead and type dress totally unlike its familiar make-up. It had been printed with the mechanical facilities of the *Gold Hill News,* which Alf Doten, with characteristic generosity, had placed at the disposal of his displaced rival for the duration of the emergency. In the issue of the twenty-eighth the paper's offices were listed as being with Driscoll & Tritle, stockbrokers, at the southeast corner of C and Taylor streets. Taylor Street formed the precise southern boundary of the destroyed portion of town.

From these temporary business offices, THE ENTERPRISE removed the next day to the paint store of J. Frederick one door south of its brief *pied-à-terre* with Driscoll & Tritle, whose senior partner, Tritle, shortly left the Comstock to become Governor of Arizona.

On November 16 THE ENTERPRISE resumed its original four-page format and familiar typeset at the same time announcing that its offices were in Odd Fellow's Hall and in its news columns telling of the purchase of an entire new printing plant to be installed presently at the old address, 24 South C Street. The same issue stated that the *Weekly Enterprise* was to be resumed at once and editorially thanked Alf Doten, "a private relief committee of one," for the generous loan of office space, type, and presses. In a word, the daily paper missed but a single issue and the weekly edition but three numbers.

Virginia City at the time of the Great Fire was at the very apex of its golden fortunes. Its mines were in full production and the value of its various properties, carried up with the new bonanzas of 1873, was estimated in the hundreds of millions. In these circumstances the town was rebuilt in record time, new residences, public buildings, and commercial structures arising from the ruins with a celerity which only wealth and optimism could implement. The International Hotel arose—six wonderful stories of luxury—to establish the Comstock as the Cosmopolis of the West. Open-handed John Mackay rebuilt the church of St. Mary's-in-the-Mountains in enduring stone. Mills and mine hoists reduced to ashes were redesigned with the newest and most powerful mining machinery in the world.

THE TERRITORIAL ENTERPRISE moved back into its old premises as soon as the gutted shell could be made fit for productional occupancy. It was now owned by the Bank of California under the title of the Enterprise Publishing Company, with Rollin Daggett as editor. With Sharon, now Senator, in the East and Mills preoccupied with more important ventures, supervision of the property was largely vested in Henry Yerington, General Superintendent of the also booming Virginia & Truckee Railroad and owner of wealthy acres of timber in the High Sierra.

The reported price paid by Sharon to Goodman for the newspaper in 1874 was half a million dollars. If this were so, the figure did not necessarily represent its real value as an investment but rather its worth to a very rich man anxious to acquire a political asset. No expense would have been too great to silence a paper which two years before had told its readers that a man capable of such malevolence and treachery as characterized Sharon's political methods "ought to be lashed naked from the haunts of civilization."

Even with THE ENTERPRISE in his pocket, Sharon was not without newspaper opposition on the Comstock. "He is simply the possessor of an enormous fortune with which he has already purchased the Republican machinery," snarled the *Virginia City Chronicle*. "When the people send a man to the Senate because he is rich enough to buy votes as well as his office, they must reasonably expect that he will sell them, his office and his country for money."

But the *Chronicle* was not THE ENTERPRISE and Sharon was shortly boarding the steamcars for Washington.

Goodman, also a rich man now by any standards save those of the bonanza kings, retired from the Comstock to spend the remainder of his days in the archeological pursuits toward which his scholarly nature inclined. With the passing years he seemed gradually to merge with the shadows of the past he admired to explore.

Whatever may have been the amount of the revenues from THE ENTERPRISE either during its first great years of promise or during the Comstock's later and even more fabulous bonanzas, Dennis McCarthy was no man to regard as dross the minted gold double eagles with knurled edges which were universal currency. All his life McCarthy stood and uncovered, at least metaphorically, in the presence of rich men, and the possibility that he might himself be numbered among their august company led to his selling his partnership to Goodman and taking the down stage for Montgomery Street.

This was in 1865 and McCarthy was a warm man, in the Forsytean sense of the word. The fortune he had amassed in Virginia City he invested in Comstock shares among the stock jobbers of San Francisco, just in time to be wiped out in the first of the Comstock's several successive declines into operational borrasca.

Back came luckless Dennis to Virginia City, this time not riding outside in the seat of honor next Hank Monk, but inside among the whisky salesmen and other undistinguished travelers. Goodman gave him a job setting type in the composing room of the newspaper of which but a few weeks before he had been half owner.

A decade passed and some of McCarthy's cats and dogs came to life. The Big Bonanza of 1873 carried up with it the value of shares long forgotten and gathering dust in the Tilton & McFarland patent strongbox in the front office. McCarthy was in clover again and in 1875 he purchased the *Virginia City Chronicle*, which he shortly established on a paying basis as the leading voice of Storey County Democrats. Half a century later the wheel had come full circle and the *Virginia Evening Chronicle*, itself already booked as a one-way fare to eternity, still carried the name of THE TERRITORIAL ENTERPRISE, acquired by merger, on its masthead.

Relations between THE ENTERPRISE and the *Chronicle*, although at variance politically on numerous occasions, were generally good. Now and then, however, they beat each other savagely about the ears while the Comstock made book on the outcome.

Upon one such occasion, Rollin Daggett, by now editor in chief of THE ENTERPRISE, was engaged in a feud of Montague-Capulet dimensions with the *Chronicle* over the policy of Southern reconstruction being followed by the administration at Washington. He wound up editorial crossbows with ferocious sneers and their quarrels whizzed about McCarthy's ears as he cowered in the offices of the *Chronicle* down the street.

One gelid winter night Daggett rolled into the editorial rooms in a condition he liked to describe as "taut," and admitted with enthusiasm that he had looked long and lovingly on the decanter of Steamboat gin, his favorite restorative, at The Old Magnolia.

He had encountered an old-time printer who had worked for the now legendary J. West Goodwin of the *Sedalia Bazoo*, whose high white beaver hat and lurid political opinions had made him a Missouri celebrity. Goodwin made a profitable sideline out of running excursions to public executions. He chartered special trains and ran up handbills advertising "Great Gala Multiple Hanging, Everyone Come" and transported thousands at two dollars a head to the scene of revelry. He had also invented Goodwin's Patent Liquor Cure, which consisted of his buying a ten-gallon keg of whisky and, every time he took a drink, of replacing it with the same amount of water. "By the time all the liquor is gone and there's nothing left but water, I'll no longer want liquor," he asserted. The cure never worked.

Daggett had left the printer and the barkeep harmonizing a composing room song called "Slug Fourteen," with the stanza:

> He leaned upon the stone and swore:
> By Jesus Christ as I have said before
> And you have often, often heard me tell
> Brevier won't justify with nonpareil.

Daggett now purposed to have at McCarthy with poisoned arrows.

Daggett, whom Wells Drury was later to characterize as "the Cyrano de Bergerac of Comstock journalism," busied himself with pen and paper for an hour or so and then suggested to Judge Goodwin at the adjacent desk that they go see if the printer was still singing. They could ask him to hot oysters and Steamboat at Chapman's Chop House, an all-night resort in North B Street.

Goodwin, always prudent and conciliatory, paused in reaching for his Inverness to look over Daggett's copy and what he saw horrified him. It was a personal attack on McCarthy such as hadn't been written since the epigrams of Catullus.

"If you run that leader, McCarthy will get his gun in the morning and fill you full of buckshot," Goodwin protested.

"You think so?" Daggett asked with alcoholic cunning.

"I do indeed," said Goodwin.

"Then I'll fix that," Daggett leered. "I'll get up real early in the morning and tell him you wrote it!"

The article was run and Goodwin listened intently from a handy place of refuge in The Delta for sounds of gunfire from the offices of THE ENTERPRISE. None came. Late that evening, boiled as owls, Daggett and McCarthy rolled into The Delta arm in arm. They had been dining together at Barnum's and had destroyed a case of Mumm's Extra while demolishing a marinated antelope.

On another occasion there was a dispute in THE ENTERPRISE editorial

THE ENTERPRISE WAS EVERYWHERE

"Charles H. Fosgard, an engineer of the C & C shaft, committed suicide at 9:30 last evening, shooting himself through the head with a
Colt's Navy revolver while seated in a game of farobank in the Sawdust
Saloon. Mr. Fosgard seems to have been suffering for a long time from
that fearful depression which sometimes seizes people in this section. It
is particularly severe in persons of certain temperament and is very apt
to increase with time." The Territorial Enterprise, January 29, 1879.

By rare good fortune a reporter for The Enterprise was present at this
melancholy occasion and able to supply details for an artist of the *Police
Gazette*, in which this picture appeared three weeks later. The "suicide
table" is still visible at the Sawdust Corner Saloon in Virginia City, just
as it was that fatal night.

sanctum about the spelling of a word and Daggett, who boasted of his lexicography, reached for a dictionary to prove his point.

"I'd rather be right than be President!" he said grandly.

"That's the way we all feel about you, Rollin," replied Judge Goodwin mildly. Daggett let out an anguished scream and spent fifteen minutes trying vainly to borrow his gun from each of the editors present, claiming loudly that murder was justified and acquittal certain upon provocation of that sort.

Another story well illustrates the occasional barbaric ferocity of Rollin Daggett.

One of the fascinating conjectures of American newspaper history concerns what paper was first to print the story of the Custer massacre at the Little Big Horn, on June 25, 1876. Legend has it that a mysterious account, said to be based on Indian smoke signals, came over the night wire to the offices of the *Sioux City* (Iowa) *Journal* four or five days before the steamer *Far West* arrived at Bismarck July 5 with the terrible details. The telegraph editor held in his hand a beat of world dimensions but, being in wine, failed to note the names and numbers involved and buried the item in a five-line paragraph of state news. Not until the *Far West* landed, and C. A. Lounsberry, editor of the *Bismarck Tribune*, was roused from bed to start wiring the sensational story to the Associated Press, did it horrify the entire world with its impact.

Details of the massacre came over the night wire to THE ENTERPRISE on July 6 and Judge Goodwin silently handed the yellow page to Daggett. His reaction shocked the conservative Goodwin beyond measure.

"Big fellows," roared Daggett, his eyes flashing, admiration in his voice. "Roman noses, fighters those Sioux! I'm proud of them!"

Himself one of the earliest of all Argonauts, Daggett had faced the Western wilderness with no properties to his name other than an army blanket and a Sharps rifle, and it was proverbial on the *Golden Era*, where he first landed a job, that he was half savage when aroused.

One day Daggett met William Sharon outside the International and the Senator asked him to have breakfast with him while discussing a matter of policy. Daggett protested that he had already breakfasted but would have a glass of something for his stomach. Sharon, a dainty eater, commanded broiled quail and a pint of claret and Daggett called the waiter back and ordered a "miner's special," a large sirloin steak garnished with fried eggs, and a bottle of Steamboat.

"But I thought you'd had breakfast," protested Sharon.

"I had, but the way you eat makes me hungry," replied THE ENTER-PRISE editor.

"I'd give half my fortune for your appetite," remarked Sharon, un-wisely pursuing the subject.

"Yes," said Daggett, "and the other half for my nobility of character and youthful figure."

Goodwin, describing Daggett, remarked that "he had no more form than a sack of apples and his character, from a Christian standpoint, was a good deal shopworn in spots."

One of the Comstock lawyers, General Thomas Williams, who had recently made $12,000,000 in Con-Virginia was seized with a hanker for the United States Senate, then regarded as the world's most exclusive club of millionaires. All the nabobs, Fair, Sharon, Jones, and Stewart were senators, and Williams, too, pined for the toga.

Daggett promptly wrote an editorial based on information about the General's private life, "calculated," as Judge Goodwin later said, "to de-press his hopes of success."

The General inspected the caps on the nipples of his Colt's dragoon revolver to confront Daggett and in almost uncontrollable rage demanded his authority for the libel.

"Oh," said Daggett, recoiling from the muzzle of the General's gun as from a puff adder and making conciliatory motions with both hands, "I had the story from Peters," naming a not-too-bright lawyer of their common acquaintance.

Williams departed in search of the culprit Peters, who shortly, white and shaken, appeared at THE ENTERPRISE. The palsied man of law de-manded of Daggett why he had told such an infamous lie.

"It's this way," said Daggett soothingly. "The General burst in sudden-like and most intemperate of speech. Threatened to shoot me, in fact. I had to pass the buck to someone and you were the first son of a bitch that came to mind."

That life on the Comstock had only slightly abated its overtones of gunfire in the 'eighties is suggested by two items from the papers of the period:

This morning about 8 o'clock, as the passengers from San Francisco were awaiting the starting of the V & T train for Virginia, two men got into an argument in front of Chamberlain's saloon. One of them was a tall man and the other a short one, the big fellow called the small one a liar, and the small one responded with a blow on the nose of the big fellow. Then the big man drew a pistol and shot the other in the belly. The wounded man walked around for half an hour, and when the train left he was walking off with a doctor in search of a drug store, complaining of feeling badly. The general impression among the passengers is that the man was fatally hurt.

Friday evening, about dark, a bullet entered the residence of Henry Potter, South H Street, narrowly missing some members of the family. The ball was of large size, apparently that of a musket, or one of the new styles of patent cartridge pistols. It passed through a north window of the kitchen, showering bits of glass upon a paper which Mr. Potter was reading and into the hair of a child he was holding on his lap, then struck an iron pot standing on the stove at which Mrs. Potter was cooking, when it fell flattened into a pan in which a beefsteak was being cooked. Before striking the pot it cut a piece out of the lower sleeve of Mrs. Potter's dress. Where the bullet came from was a mystery, and the Potter family hope that no one is angry at them.

Nor, apparently, did a rising tide of sports interest materially diminish the business of the two hundred saloons which by this time flourished in Virginia and its suburbs. The following items appeared in the same issue of the paper and in appropriate proximity.

"I hereby challenge Ed. Cummings to run me from 100 to 150 yards for $200 a side—the race to take place between this date and the 10th of December. Man and money can be found at Gold Hill with $50 forfeit ready at any time." C. V. Burns.

"I accept the challenge of C. V. Burns to run 150 yards, but the small amount of the stakes would not justify me to quit drinking and go into training. I therefore refuse to run for less than $500." Ed. Cummings.

William Crowhurst of San Francisco, Grand Lecturer of the Independent Order of Good Templars, will give free lectures tomorrow and Thursday evenings at the Presbyterian Church. Mr. Crowhurst is at present on a lecturing tour throughout the State under the auspices of the Grand Lodge of California. He has been advised that there is a great field here for temperance work.

Nectar Sour Mash Whiskey, the cream of the distiller's art, is ripe, old and mellow. Every trial bottle gains a new friend. Quart bottles, 50 cents, 75 cents and $1.00 according to age. At McGurn's Store, South C Street.

That THE ENTERPRISE could still as in the old days make or break Nevada politicians more or less at will was demonstrated in the case of Governor Luther R. Bradley, well, if not altogether favorably, known as "Old Broadhorns." Bradley, a blundering 200-pound cattleman, had no qualifications for office, a circumstance which seldom militates against election in Nevada, had served two terms without provoking catastrophe on the commonwealth, and purposed to run again in 1878.

At the instigation of some of the boss-haters of the time and place, he announced that his platform would be a mighty tax on all bullion produced within the state and a tax on all corporations doing business in Nevada for the full amount of their capital stock at par. Such legislation would have wrecked the economy of the state in a matter of minutes and closed every mine on the Comstock with absolute finality.

There was nothing left for Goodwin but to destroy the Governor. Day after day THE ENTERPRISE beat the old man around the ears with bladders, threw banana peels in his path on the sidewalk, and smashed his plug hat with snowballs. Whenever he attempted to take a firm stand, THE ENTERPRISE jerked the rug out from under him. In his attempts at rebuttal the old gentleman fell down political coal holes and was perpetually "it" in a hilarious game of blind man's buff. He didn't stand a chance. The Democrats, horrified at the carnage they had precipitated, stayed away from the polls and refused to show their faces on election day. The Republicans poleaxed the Governor and retired him from Nevada politics forever.

A short time later Bradley died, assassinated as his friends said by THE ENTERPRISE, and Goodwin, although suffering from no such delusions of guilt, felt badly about the old fellow for the rest of his days. "Sometimes an honest newspaper has to present things in such a light," he said, "as makes everyone connected with it wish he could avoid the duty."

With Goodwin, more than with most ENTERPRISE editors, such protestations of distaste were creditable. He was incapable of cynicism. Shortly after this Judge Goodwin resigned as editor of THE ENTERPRISE to go to the *Salt Lake Tribune*. His last appearance on the Comstock was when he was asked to return for a municipal celebration in 1909, but he was so enfeebled that many who had assembled to do honor to a grand old man from the legendary past were disappointed at being unable to hear his voice.

During the 'nineties the principal source of income for both THE ENTERPRISE and the *Chronicle*, the two remaining papers on the Lode, derived from delinquent sales insertions for Nevada mining stocks and each paper maintained an agent in San Francisco for the purpose of soliciting this business at its source. Although the insertion rate for this type of advertising was regulated by Nevada law at a much lower figure, the two papers by mutual agreement kept the rate for delinquent stock sales at $2.00 per square, a square being twelve column-width lines of nonpareil. This, in the currency of the time, was a rate described as extortionate and it alone, in all probability, kept the two papers alive as long as they lasted.

Salaries of printers thirty years after the paper's beginnings were just what they had been in the 'sixties: sixty-five cents per thousand ems of type, most of which was six point solid which a good compositor could set at the rate of a thousand an hour. Pressmen received $6.00 a day. The composition rate of pay put a high premium on clean typeset as well as on speed because, on a space-rate computation, the printer received no pay for correcting from proof.

Until the advent of the first linotype, THE ENTERPRISE mechanical staff comprised five compositors and an apprentice, a city editor, and a business manager who at one time lived in the apartment upstairs in the Enterprise Building and had proofs of all matter sent up to him in a dumb waiter throughout the night, catching sleep as he could between galleys. Its arrival in the waiter was announced by a piercing whistle. The press was operated by the foreman of the mechanical department and hand-fed by the apprentice.

Five printers, as the fortunes of the paper were approaching their nadir and its circulation had declined to less than 400, was one more than was required, but as one of them could be relied on at any given time to be drunk and incapable of holding a stick, the force really only numbered four.

In 1894 the first linotype in any newspaper west of the Mississippi was installed in THE ENTERPRISE composing room and the staff of printers reduced to one. Darius Ogden Mills, the San Francisco moneybags, had been surprised one morning to discover the paper's portfolio among his properties where it had been slipped by Senator Sharon when its usefulness in achieving the toga for him was ended. Mills was one of the largest stockholders in the newly organized Mergenthaler Linotype Company. THE ENTERPRISE seemed a good place to try the machine out.

In Farnsworth's time the foreman was an erudite and scholarly student of Latin and the classical humanities named John Plant, who had been with the paper since the days of Joe Goodman. After five in the afternoon Plant was inclined to be in wine and the staff knew the old man's precise alcohol content by the ferocity with which he tugged at a huge pair of handlebar mustaches. If he pulled them so fiercely that they seemed about to shift their moorings they knew him to be uncommonly mellow.

Joe Farnsworth estimated that the steam press of THE ENTERPRISE in the 'sixties and 'seventies, running two pages up, could print few more

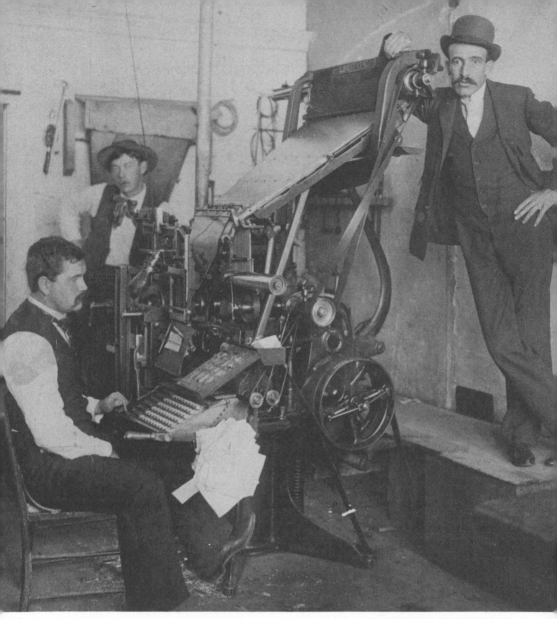

THE SHAPE OF THINGS TO COME

FIRST LINOTYPE in any newspaper shop west of the Mississippi was installed in THE ENTERPRISE in 1894. At its console is Frank Blake, then a compositor, later the paper's publisher. Standing in the rear is Joe Farnsworth, then apprentice and soon to be Nevada State Printer, and leaning against the primal machine in the cast-iron derby that was the trademark of his calling, is H. P. Remington, old-time itinerant printer whose profession was to be rendered obsolete by Mergenthaler.

than 1,000 impressions an hour, which, counting the second run for the remaining two pages of a four-page paper, accounts for 1,000 complete copies every two hours. Press time was at two in the morning and the delivery boys were called for six. With no closer data from which to compute, this would indicate that the press run of the paper was in the neighborhood of 2,000. By 1893, Farnsworth estimated, the circulation was a mere 350.

The sound of THE ENTERPRISE press rumbling in the midnight basement, he said, could be heard for several blocks and competed on terms of equality with the noises of the stamp mills and mine hoists.

THE ENTERPRISE suspended publication January 15, 1893, but by December of that year the property had been leased to John E. McKinnon, who had until then been a printer on the *Chronicle*.

McKinnon was another ENTERPRISE editor with a genius for attracting catastrophe. Within two years of taking over he unleashed his editorial bloodhounds on the trail of Francis G. Newlands, then an aspirant for congress on the Democratic ticket. It was highly injudicious, as Newlands was well connected both in Nevada and in San Francisco, not to mention his being son-in-law of Senator Sharon himself. It is only charitable to suppose McKinnon had a temporary lapse from sanity.

Henry Yerington, superintendent of the Virginia & Truckee Railroad, a partner in many profitable ventures with Sharon and the Bank of California's hatchet man on the Comstock, read THE ENTERPRISE at breakfast and knew just what to do. He didn't even get Montgomery Street on the telephone but ordered an engine from the roundhouse coupled to his business car, told the dispatcher to give him the railroad all the way to Virginia, and was streaking through Empire and Mound House within half an hour.

McKinnon, the human lightning rod, was out of a job ten minutes after the super's special had ground to a stop in the depot. He had $4.65 in his pocket and a sick wife and was last heard of setting type for the *Oakland Tribune*. His departure was the last major editorial excitement of THE ENTERPRISE in the nineteenth century.

Successors to McKinnon were Frank Blake, a former compositor, and John Craise, a printer, who took over as the lights of the Comstock were growing dim and THE ENTERPRISE itself was starting its long decline into eventual borrasca.

Coda In Bold Face

HE TERRITORIAL ENTERPRISE awoke from its long sleep in 1951. To the casual eye its sleep had been practically indistinguishable from death, but the authors of its reactivation thought they detected in its still magic name some traces of vital pulse.

The International Hotel and the Virginia & Truckee Railroad were gone beyond all recall because their being had been altogether tangible, and once their properties were vanished they were forever with yesterday.

But THE TERRITORIAL ENTERPRISE was at once a name, a legend, and an impulse of vitality in whose economy presses and ink were incidentals that could be supplied, and shortly were.

From the time of its suspension as an active and independent newspaper property in 1916, THE TERRITORIAL ENTERPRISE had existed in a state of suspended animation in other Comstock newspapers. As late as 1920 its name appeared in the standing matter of the *Virginia Evening Chronicle*, in the editorship of L. N. Clark. Its good will, subscription list, and advertising had been absorbed by the *Chronicle*, which was printed in a decrepit premises six doors down the street from THE ENTERPRISE' old stand, but its machinery and fixtures remained in their place gathering rust and cobwebs as the years passed.

The combined *Evening Chronicle* and the ghostly ENTERPRISE limped wearily down the decades together until August 6, 1927, when Virginia City could no longer support a daily and the *Chronicle* bade its predecessors move over in the graveyard and itself crept quietly to rest. Comstockers are still able to evoke a mild indignation over the fate of the *Chronicle*'s press and other mechanical resources which were purchased by a well-heeled Montana rancher who happened to be passing through and set up a thousand miles or so away with a sign reading "Original Plant of the *Virginia City Evening Chronicle*." The place was Virginia City, Montana.

The week following the demise of the *Chronicle* its assets, including the name of THE TERRITORIAL ENTERPRISE, were merged in the *Monday Budget*—whose life span under J. T. Huling was less than three years—and then Vincent Nevin bought Huling out in the name of a weekly to be known as the *Virginia City News*. It is doubtful by this time if, in the disorder of their affairs, the various and successive heirs to the name of THE ENTERPRISE even realized it was part of their property. Until 1951 its name was discontinued altogether on the mastheads of the *Budget* and *News*.

But though the vein of ore had been lost at the head of the drift it was nevertheless there for anyone possessed of the urge to follow it, and in the fall of 1951 the present proprietors of the property took an option on the *Virginia City News*, the weekly "voice of Storey County" with a circulation, at the most optimistic guess, of fewer than 200. The agreement called for them to take over active management of the paper from the Virginia Printing Company of Sparks, a suburb of Reno, the following May.

The name of THE TERRITORIAL ENTERPRISE, after a lapse of thirty years while its files gathered dust in the libraries of the West, was at once reestablished in the editorial page masthead and standing matter of the *News*, and specifically named among the assets of that paper in the agreement of its purchase. Minted gold changed hands for the name.

The combined TERRITORIAL ENTERPRISE & VIRGINIA CITY NEWS appeared on schedule May 2, 1952. Tabloid in form, five columns of fourteen-inch typeset to the page, the first issue established continuity with the old ENTERPRISE where it had left off in 1916 as Volume 98, No. 18. Its first issue was distributed in the dusk of a spring evening by Charlie Addis, by now dean of the town's characters and seventy-eight-year-old newsboy who, thirty-six years before, had distributed the last copies of THE ENTERPRISE the night its presses fell silent, presumably forever. The masthead listed Charles Clegg and Lucius Beebe as sole owners in partnership, the former in the capacity of editor, the latter as publisher.

Widespread publicity and generous editorial acclaim greeted the reappearance of one of the atmospheric properties of the Old West. From coast to coast, from the *Oregonian* to the *New York Herald Tribune* and from the *Deseret News* to the *New Orleans Times-Picayune*, editors searched the musty files and came up with editorials of welcome and felicitation. All the wire services carried extended stories and features shortly began to flourish in Sunday sections and national periodicals, and have never ceased. Almost alone, the *Christian Science Monitor* seemed to take a dim view of rebirth at Virginia City.

Entirely aware of the uses of publicity, the owners of THE ENTERPRISE had prepared specially written and assembled "package job" releases aimed at the particular editorial preferences and economies of a number of im-

THE ENTERPRISE RIDES AGAIN

IN 1952 THE TERRITORIAL ENTERPRISE was restored and reactivated as
a weekly newspaper by Lucius Beebe and Charles Clegg. Beebe, who
assumed the office of publisher, had for twenty-one years been a member
of the editorial staff of the *New York Herald Tribune* in that newspaper's
golden age, when members of its staff included such radiant names as
Percy Hammond, W. O. McGeehan, Stanley Walker, Alva Johnston, and
Franklin P. Adams. Clegg was a photographer of note and collaborator
with Beebe in numerous books of railroading and Western Americana.
The partners purchased the faltering *Virginia City News*, repository
through a long succession of mergers and abandonments of the name
of THE TERRITORIAL ENTERPRISE, and in May 1952, after gathering dust
in the files for thirty-six years, Nevada's by now legendary newspaper
reappeared on the streets of Virginia City. Here Editor Charles Clegg
and Publisher Lucius Beebe examine the first press run with Joseph
McDonald, publisher of the *Nevada State Journal*.

portant newspapers and magazines. Among them was a potential editorial page feature mailed to the Boston offices of the *Christian Science Monitor*, an organ notable for its good works and high spiritual *ton*. The feature aimed at the *Monitor* was sedulous in its abatement of mention of Nevada institutions of which the editors of the paper were sure not to approve. It dwelt lovingly upon Mark Twain and THE ENTERPRISE' fair repute as an agency of enlightenment and belles lettres. No mention was made of Virginia City's twenty flourishing saloons or the circumstance that the paper's major source of revenue was gambling in Reno and Las Vegas. In most newspaper offices, where hundreds of such releases are received each mail, those unsuited to publication are relegated briskly to the wastebasket. Not so the *Monitor*. The story of THE ENTERPRISE' rise from the dead came back with practically the speed of light, with no comment but by air mail. The new tycoons of Nevada's Fleet Street thought they were able to detect on its margins marks where, in the *Monitor's* offices, it had been handled with firetongs.

On the Comstock itself, a substantial number of residents and businessmen were and still are determinedly indifferent to the existence of THE ENTERPRISE. There are in Virginia City a number of subscribers to the Indian religious rite of suttee, in which the widow follows her husband to the funeral pyre in a gesture of ultimate immolation, and a number of old-timers felt that the community should be allowed to dissolve into final nothingness along with the fortunes of the mines that had brought it into being. The hand was impious that sought to stay communal suicide.

Then, too, the newspaper itself was like nothing they had ever encountered among the miasmic everglades of Nevada weekly journalism. THE ENTERPRISE didn't carry Dagwood or Popeye and for reasons of its own, obscure and possibly subversive, didn't devote extended front-page space to the meetings of the Rebekahs. Furthermore it had a formal editorial page, a pretension to grandeur indulged in by no other Nevada weekly, on which no patent medicine advertising was sold and in whose columns actual opinions seemed to be expressed. This was obviously against God, as no other Nevada newspaper of any sort had in recent years entertained an editorial idea other than that baby, mother, and the Flag were good things and that the public school system deserved the support of the taxpayers. Beyond this the dictates of prudence did not extend.

Virginia City, with a few radiantly notable exceptions, flatly refused to take advertising space in THE ENTERPRISE and its proprietors were forced to alter their over-all approach to make the paper more a weekly of the

HEIR TO THE MANTLE OF JOE GOODMAN

CHARLES CLEGG, Editor of THE ENTERPRISE in its ninety-fifth year, shown with a friend, Nevada's Governor Vail Pittman. A direct descendant of Miles Standish of Pilgrim Fathers fame, Clegg, besides editing THE ENTERPRISE, is a confirmed motor car enthusiast and racing driver. The week after he had editorially urged the harshest treatment at the law's discretion for hot-rodders who hurrah the Comstock, he purchased an imported, snow-white Jaguar racing car warranted to achieve 115 miles an hour. "It proves my tolerance and versatility," he said grandly, integrating the car to the editorial. "Besides, I hear that driving a Jaguar is, in the vernacular, ecstatically george." Two nights later, when the Editor of THE ENTERPRISE was arrested and fined $20 for disturbing the peace with his unmuffled horsepower and exceeding the Virginia City speed limit by seventy miles an hour, the press of the nation was happy over the event. "Either it proves the power of the press," *Newsweek* quoted Clegg as saying, "or it proves that the press has no power at all. I don't know which."

West and of Nevada as a whole, rather than of the unresponsive Comstock.

Things got off to a start after a fashion.

There were initial misunderstandings. A news story in an early issue had occasion to speak fair words about the District Attorney for Storey County and the next mail brought a demand, couched in terms of legal outrage, from the D.A.'s law partner demanding a retraction, and that instanter.

Since the mention had been altogether flattering and reflected nothing on the blameless reputation of the man of law, THE ENTERPRISE owners were surprised. Inquiry revealed that nobody had ever before had occasion to speak with anything even remotely approximating favor of the incumbent of the district attorney's office. It was with difficulty that the man of writs and injunctions was convinced that the mention hadn't been "writ sarcastic."

Virginia City in the mid-twentieth century is still the scene of low and joyous commotions whose chronicling would raise the hair, like porcupines at Doomsday, on editorial heads in more inhibited newspaper offices. Its owners simply look to the past for precedent.

A long tradition of outrage hasn't been wholly abated by the devisings of propriety. Stabbings, embezzlements, defalcations, nose pasting and the burning of powder are regular enough occurrences, especially in summer months, to keep the columns of THE TERRITORIAL ENTERPRISE from too closely resembling the *Christian Science Monitor*.

When a paragraph reported that the good ladies of the Altar Society of St. Mary's-in-the-Mountains, having spent the evening in holy precincts mapping good works, unanimously sought refreshment after labor in the Sky Deck Saloon, there was a tornado of protest from the good ladies. They hadn't gone to the Sky Deck at all; they had spent the shank of the evening at the Old Capitol.

When John Byrne, the night constable on duty outside the Sazarac, had emptied his gun after a fleeing carload of hot rodders bent on hurrahing the town and had succeeded only in shattering the front window of Greer's tearoom and narrowly missed maiming Olive Lane when she put her head out of the Old Mr. Comstock Bar to see what, quite literally, all the shooting was about, he was gently questioned about his marksmanship at the next meeting of the Board of Storey County Supervisors. Had the night constable possibly been drinking while on duty? "Since we got rid of the girls on the Divide, what the hell else is there to do at night?" was

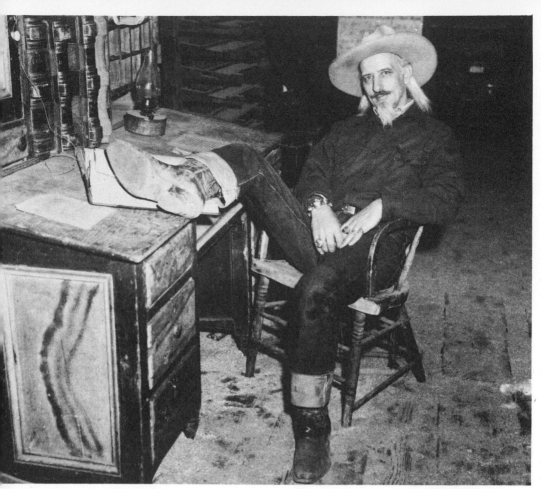

BUFFALO BILL IN C STREET

INFORMALLY SHOWN at the Mark Twain desk in the Mark Twain
Museum in THE TERRITORIAL ENTERPRISE Building, at 24A South C
Street, is Roy Shetler, proprietor of everything in sight and custodian
of many tangible souvenirs of the fragrant past. Although Mark Twain
shared with Dan De Quille a deal table in the composing room and
wrote much of his ENTERPRISE copy handy to the type cases, the desk
does indeed date from his time in the office and may very well have been
used by him on occasion. Its almost precise counterpart, also designated
as "Mark Twain's desk," is in the History Room of the Wells Fargo Bank
& Union Trust Company in San Francisco. The Mark Twain Museum is
located in the one-time pressroom of THE ENTERPRISE and includes
among its properties the Series 1 Linotype, the first west of the Mississippi,
which was installed in 1894, a water-powered flat bed press on which
the paper was once printed, and a job press of unknown antecedents but
of so mature a vintage that experts profess to see marks of Indian warfare
on it.

the answer. Confronted with irrefutable logic the commissioners hastily dropped the matter.

By reason as much of their durability and professional acquaintance with the outer world as by virtue of the status of THE ENTERPRISE, its publisher and editor came to be an unofficial reception committee for the entertainment of distinguished visitors to the Comstock. If Cole Porter or Messmore Kendall, Sophie Tucker, Irving Berlin, Nunnally Johnson, Seymour Weiss, Dave Chasen or Stanton Delaplane are in town, it is taken for granted that they lunch or dine with THE ENTERPRISE.

Ward Morehouse, columnist of the *New York World Telegram & Sun*, once drove directly to Virginia City from Jack & Charlie's in West Fifty-second Street to bring the publisher a firkin of fresh caviar and thereafter made a practice of visiting Nevada for a week or so each summer. "The moral tone of Virginia City is so low that it's one place in the world where I'm not conspicuous," he says.

San Francisco's celebrated barrister Jake Ehrlich seldom misses an opportunity to invite THE ENTERPRISE to leave its professional duties and come across the street to The Delta. Luminaries of letters, Stewart Holbrook, Oscar Lewis, Vincent Sheean, and Roger Butterfield find company in the editors of the Comstock. Visiting magazine and newspaper writers by the score find the latchstring in its conventional place.

Sometimes their devotion to the interests of the property leads the owners of THE ENTERPRISE into extended symposiums with visiting celebrities. One such a while back was Ralph Champion, head of the American bureau of the *London Daily Mirror*, which boasts the largest circulation in the world. Champion arrived for lunch and three days later was returned to his suite in the Riverside Hotel in Reno.

That night a holocaust of Neronic proportions destroyed a film theater directly across the street, and the next morning his hosts in Virginia City telephoned to ascertain if Champion had enjoyed the spectacle.

"No, I didn't even get out of bed," deposed the slightly shopworn journalist. "During the night I heard a vast amount of screaming and smashing of glass and ringing of bells and what sounded like the falling of walls and such, but after three evenings in Virginia City I thought it just a part of your cheery American night life so I turned over and went back to sleep."

An Oregon lumberman, a friend of the publisher of THE ENTERPRISE, came to Virginia City to take a bride and was married in the pressroom where coolers of wine had thoughtfully been placed on the folding and delivery tables. He too remained three unforeseen days in Nevada and the departure of the bridegroom from the Balcony Suite in The Silver Dollar was chronicled in the paper as being "cheerful despite the heavy cast on a broken leg." His approach to the nuptial bower had been made in injudicious haste and he had fallen the length of a flight of stairs.

At one time and briefly in its early days of reactivation THE ENTERPRISE had a sort of tenuous bond with good works. Its general manager on part time was also part-time sacristan of St. Mary's-in-the-Mountains, Virginia City's notably beautiful and enduring Roman Catholic church.

The paper's finances were not as demanding of accountancy as they came to be later and the petty-cash drawer was conducted very much like the office cash compartment in the safe of Colonel Marse Henry Watterson of the *Louisville Courier-Journal*. Every afternoon Watterson went across the street to the Louisville Jockey Club to test his theory that "a bob-tail flush can beat a pair of deuces when the wind and the chips are in the right direction," and to finance his researches the Colonel helped himself to whatever sum seemed appropriate from petty cash, a practice which next morning caused understandable grief and consternation among the auditors. Finally the cashier prevailed upon the old gentleman to make out a requisition for whatever he abstracted. "It's your money, Colonel, but it's hard on the bookkeepers when they don't know what you've taken." Watterson assured him that in the future he would co-operate. The next morning they found the cashbox bare and a slip from the owner announced the amount he had taken. It read: "All!"

A similar formality characterized THE ENTERPRISE office cash.

Then one day during the progress of a Comstock blizzard, augmented by a snowstorm of bad checks, the man of ghostly offices disappeared, taking with him substantial sums from the poor box and numerous holy artifacts. THE ENTERPRISE was amused, within the bounds of decorum, and headlined the story

MIRACLE IN REVERSE CHANGES CHURCH FUNDS
INTO THIN AIR

When the possibilities of an even more comprehensive miracle dawned upon them, the owners of the paper investigated their own petty-cash department. As Colonel Watterson had so aptly said, it was "All."

At the outset, THE ENTERPRISE had maintained editorial rooms in the premises at 24 South C Street (to which the paper had moved in 1863), rented from Roy "Buffalo Bill" Shetler, their present owner, and the paper had been printed at job plants in Reno. The finished papers were then brought up the hill, distributed locally, and mailed from the Virginia City post office.

By the end of the first year it was apparent that this was not the solution to the paper's problems. Most Nevada weeklies in order to survive at all are of necessity family enterprises conducted on a self-contained basis and only infrequently employing union mechanics. The cost of union labor throughout would close nine out of ten of them overnight and the expense of publishing THE ENTERPRISE at a job plant removed by fifty round-trip miles from its editorial rooms was costing most of what the paper took in. The inconvenience of driving up and down to Reno for make-up and supervision was also a dismaying factor.

Spring of 1953 saw THE ENTERPRISE embark on the costly and hazardous expedient of building its own plant in Virginia City. It was the first industry of consequence to return to the Comstock instead of leaving it in more than half a century. The last mine had sealed its shaft, the last mill fallen silent, and the sole industry of the community was that of sluicing and gentling the tourist trade and selling it the Comstock past.

A completely modern stone and cement structure was built in the rear of the venerable Enterprise Building, where it would not detract from C Street's almost unbroken facade of Western false fronts. The necessary machinery was purchased from George Garcia and Harry Butler, San Francisco brokers in such matters, type cases, stone space, and storage rooms were set up and, not without serious misgivings, the owners prepared to manufacture their own product.

The first issue of the paper was scheduled to be printed in the new Virginia City plant the last week end in June. The museum-piece press, linotype, folder, type cases, and other costly and perishable items arrived from San Francisco aboard a monster truck before the roof was on the building designed to house them. So did the only solid week of snowfall of the entire winter.

The premises were dried out with blowtorches and for the first week or so were heated by a bonfire in a steel barrel which emitted, in Vesuvian quantities, smoke of a peculiar acridity.

When it was started, the press leaped into cyclonic action and snapped at about $1,000 worth of paper, which it happily tore into shreds while jumping up and down on its bedplates. The townsfolk who had gathered in glad anticipation of catastrophe were not disappointed, and slapped each other delightedly when the linotype squirted a stream of melted lead

THE NEW GALLOPING PONY OF THE PLAINS

THE PONY MIEHLE press shown above gallops through 2,000 pages an hour, four up, in the new plant of THE ENTERPRISE in Virginia City under the supervision of Mechanical Superintendent Clifford Kroeger. The paper's seventy-eight-year-old newsboy, Charlie Addis (*at left*), has been delivering the news on the Comstock since 1915. The Comstock is fond of an anecdote concerning the occasion when Addis encountered another homeward-bound ancient emerging from the portals of Clint Salmon's grocery with three loaves of bread under one arm and a half case of whisky under the other. "Whatever in the world," asked Addis, "are you going to do with all that bread?"

at the operator. Then there was static electricity, an elemental hazard which nobody had anticipated and few had ever heard of. Paper stock stuck together and refused to separate on the feeder, whole handfuls of it going down the guides and ending in shredded confusion in the machinery. The great steam press dementia of 1863 was re-created.

Garcia and Butler made soothing motions and an aged German necromancer arrived on the next plane from San Francisco. He was reputed to know all about static, and hung the Pony Miehle with Christmas tree tinsel to beguile the evil spirits. It didn't work and the power company sent sorcerer's apprentices to try mystic spells. The day the first run was scheduled and confusion had reached bedlamite proportions, the publisher and editor got to the shop in time to discover the Mergenthaler Merlin pouring boiling water from a teakettle in a wide circle around the machinery on the theory that the steam would carry off the malevolent currents of electricity.

It was then that the owners climbed on a plane and went to New Orleans where they stayed drunk a week with Owen Brennan, not caring if the paper came out or not. As soon as they left the building, everything started to work like a charm and, generally speaking, has ever since.

Staff members came and went with clocklike regularity, some hired away by deceitful rivals, cthers foundering in the sea of strong waters which perpetually ebbs and flows in C Street. On one occasion the management hired a young man for the office of managing editor whose name was Clemens and whom they intended for promotional purposes to fob off as a descendant of the original Sam. As had happened to his celebrated predecessor (but no relative) a strong east wind from the brewery smote him his first night on duty. He returned at dawn to the Silver Dollar Hotel, where he was with difficulty dissuaded by Florence Edwards, the proprietor, from tearing down the premises. He called that eminently respectable innkeeper a naughty name. "I'm not so an old bag," said Florence with dignity. "I'm a Bostonian and can prove it." The errant Clemens departed and drove his car to noisy destruction on the way down the mountain.

The management of THE ENTERPRISE never have made any pretense of immoderate temperance. Editorial conference is held daily at The Delta and the proprietors believe that their advertisers, many of whom are distillers of ardent spirits, deserve their personal patronage.

The *Denver Post* saw fit to admonish THE ENTERPRISE to ways of virtue. This proved to be a mistake that would never have happened in the days of the *Post*'s original owners, Fred Bonfils and Harry Tammen, either of whom could tell a coiled puff adder when they encountered one.

Familiar as it was with the record of the *Post* from Gene Fowler's time, when it was edited by a staff variously located in Mattie Silks' bagnio and Ed Chase's crooked gambling hell and saloon, THE ENTERPRISE editorially spat in the eye of the *Post* with such spitting that for some days to come its distinguished general manager Palmer Hoyt was to be observed taking restoratives in the bar of the Brown Palace and muttering about the folly of fooling with bear traps.

The editorial in THE ENTERPRISE read:

LOOK WHO'S TALKING

For two full generations now, both factually and metaphorically, the howling wonderment of the Queen City of Denver, the hilarious *Denver Post*, has swaggered happily through the saloons of Champa Street on the way to becoming one of the grand and gaudy institutions of the American West. Its first proprietors, the now legendary Harry Tammen and Fred Bonfils, first met in the bar of the elegantly upholstered Windsor Hotel in Larimer Street where Tammen was head barkeep. Bonfils was promoter of a lottery which narrow minded folk sometimes remarked had its suspicious aspects. Together they formed a riotous partnership that rocked Denver's sedate publishing circles on its congress gaiters and convulsed the impious with inextinguishable laughter. By a synthesis of showmanship, blackmail, ballyhoo and outrageous animal spirits they ballooned the once sickly *Post* into a multimillion dollar property. *The Post* incited the citizenry to civic tumult which on one occasion required calling out the troops. Its staff members, Gene Fowler among others, were never noted for temperance leanings and the entire atmosphere of *The Post* was one of unabashed alcoholic hooray. Its staff members had charge accounts at Jennie Rogers' love store and *The Post's* personal and editorial conduct from the day Bon and Tam took over have been characterized by such screaming and bustling of plug hats as to become an epic of low and scandalous hilarity. *The Post* possessed a genius for chaos.

This, then, is the tall tower of civic virtue that raises a disapproving eyebrow in the direction of Virginia City and THE TERRITORIAL ENTERPRISE when Nevada's oldest newspaper asserts that culture and the humanities are strongly bonded in the cup that cheers. "THE ENTERPRISE," says *The Post* with haughty sniffs, "gets well out on a limb with the declaration that 'the consumption of liquor in its various form has, throughout recorded history, been the most reliable index of intelligence, gentility and civilization generally.'"

Having thus repudiated every flattering qualification that might apply to itself, *The Post* braces itself firmly against the mahogany and waves a palsied finger to admonish that "it might be a sound notion for THE ENTERPRISE to come out of its alcoholic haze and seek an answer to the time honored questions: whither are we drifting and whence are we bound?"

The spectacle of *The Post* thus reaching metaphorically for the cloves and coffee beans before being helped to a cab by the waiters is hilarious enough without further elaboration.

But pause!

It may be that with the passing of time and the corruption of its liver and other essentials, *The Denver Post* has removed its editorial rooms from the front parlor of Mattie Silks' bagnio in Holladay Street to the nearest Y.M.C.A. It may have issued a recall to its staff to vacate the Ships Bar in the Brown Palace in favor of more refining precincts.

Peek under those swinging doors and get a load of who's preaching temperance!

Shortly thereafter an item appeared in Abel Green's weekly *Variety*, the bible of the entertainment world:

BEEBE ON SKOLSKY

Gotham newspapermen are passing around the blistering editorial Lucius Beebe wrote in his TERRITORIAL ENTERPRISE & VIRGINIA CITY NEWS (Nev.) re Sidney Skolsky. He took the columnist to task for having "recently remarked in print without, as far as we know, provocation, that the publisher of THE TERRITORIAL ENTERPRISE was, at some unnamed date, involved in a fistfight in a Hollywood resort 'with patrons after making some insulting remarks.' " Whereupon Beebe made his points, denying having ever been "in a quarrel, brawl or altercation of any description in and around Hollywood or any Los Angeles restaurant, saloon, nightclub or similar resort . . ."

The rest of it is very heated as regards Beebe's attitude towards Skolsky—certainly one of the strongest yet in recent years, especially about personalities in the show biz–literati belt.

Among other assets inherited by the latter proprietors of THE ENTERPRISE was a willingness to tangle with all and any comers, preferably those of exalted pretensions to good works or elevated public conduct. They have never subscribed to the notion that a newspaper's obligation is to the public and Charles Clegg, its editor, has been known to be actively ill at mention of the phrase "public service." "When I have a message," he says, quoting Humphrey Bogart, "I send for Western Union."

Such sentiments have reduced to a minimum invitations for the owners of the paper to address women's clubs, civic groups, and other allied agencies of right thinking. Instructors in schools of journalism and seminaries for the impressionable young usually take steps to prevent THE ENTERPRISE from the groves of suburban academe, but its stock is in continuous ascendancy among impious contemporaries.

The conduct of business in THE ENTERPRISE office, interrupted as it frequently is by excursions of the entire staff to The Delta or Crystal for nutrition, is informal to a degree bewildering to wage slaves in more prudent establishments. On one occasion Herb Caen, the ranking San Francisco columnist in the *Examiner*, was able to report that instead of the printed exhortations to THINK which some employers distribute where the serfs can see them, the management of THE ENTERPRISE had strewn the editorial and business offices with cards advising the staff to SMIRK, SNEER, CONSPIRE, PLOT, DECEIVE, GLOAT, CONNIVE, LEER, and DEFAME.

"*Bully*" was Mr. Caen's comment.

School of journalism professors averted their gaze.

As the year 1953 neared its end it also approached the ninety-fifth anniversary of that cold and cheerless day in Mormon Station when its primal founders had pulled the first copy of Nevada's first newspaper from a frozen hand press, and the present inheritors of its name planned to observe the birthday.

"It isn't really our ninety-fifth birthday of continued operation," Clegg told the Associated Press. "The paper existed to be sure for a number of years in a state of suspended animation, but that's a condition characteristic of its owners part of the time, too. I'd say the continuity was perfect."

Messages of good will arrived in South C Street from President Eisenhower, Elder Statesman Bernard Baruch, Nevada's Governor Charles Russell, William Randolph Hearst, Jr., whose grandfather had made the first of many fortunes in Virginia City, and other notables whose names made news. The paper's owners, who frown upon annoying friends and advertisers for paid expressions of esteem on slight provocation, ran a twenty-four-page paper rather than a huge and padded special and called it a day.

They felt warm and good about things generally.

The anniversary inspired feature articles in Sunday editions as distantly separated as San Francisco, Los Angeles, Boston, and Manchester, New Hampshire. The Associated Press wired a picture story to all its feature subscribers and the American Society for State and Local History came through with a citation of merit for THE ENTERPRISE' contribution to the regional history of Nevada.

The paper's old friend, the *Oregonian*, with Stewart Holbrook at the editorial fonts, joined the here's-how chorus:

THE VOICE OF THE COMSTOCK

In the lively ghost town of Virginia City, Nevada, last week, the hardy citizenry were drinking toasts to their famous newspaper, THE TERRITORIAL ENTERPRISE, which had just passed its ninety-fifth milestone; while the mails brought birthday congratulations from President Eisenhower and many another, including Bernard Baruch who in younger days was a prospector in Nevada. To these felicitations *The Oregonian* is happy to add its own, along with wishes for another ninety-five.

For almost two years now, THE ENTERPRISE has been a rambunctious though always well-written weekly that doubtless has given its home town more fetching publicity than has been the case with much larger cities and newspapers, a condition of affairs that came about when Lucius Beebe and Charles Clegg took over the obsolescent journal and turned it into a clearly seductive voice, singing of the Comstock's current wonders and reminding readers of its stormy and elegant past.

THE ENTERPRISE knows well enough that Virginia City cannot exist save by the bounty of visitors, and to entice them the paper devotes its every effort, not by conventional boosterism but by reporting faithfully every homely event in the region—a winning run at roulette in the Delta saloon, the sudden departure of a prominent citizen in a blizzard of bad checks, and the deplorable theft of a fine electric sign from the premises of a suburban bordello.

That this kind of advertising is effective has become increasingly clear. During the past season the town was constantly overrun by happy visitors who wanted to see first-hand a community as different as possible from their own. That they came from 48 states and several foreign countries was no surprise to the circulation manager of THE ENTERPRISE, who has sworn before the Audit Bureau of Circulations that his subscribers not only are legion but are to be found in most parts of the known world.

The continuity which has been established between THE TERRITORIAL ENTERPRISE of the mid-twentieth century and its ancestral property is more than superficial. Its proprietors are urgently aware of a heritage of what Bernard De Voto calls "being West," a heritage possessed of implications of spaciousness and individualism either in partial or complete eclipse in less favored parts of the world.

As it was in the days of Joe Goodman and Rollin Daggett, it is perhaps the least formally conducted newspaper office in the land. The earliest chroniclers of THE ENTERPRISE' destinies remarked on the close affinity between editorial policy and food and drink so that a paid-up subscription was celebrated in early times with beefsteak, and a job print order with rejoicing among the pots. It requires today but the most microscopic provocation for all hands to shut up shop and repair to a tavern to celebrate a new advertising contract or other happy omen. It is not ascertainably true that the office manager, Mrs. Cecelia Andrews, and the managing editor, Fay Fuller, are unable to open the morning's mail until they have consulted the oracle of Martini, but it is in the record that no major decision either in editorial or business office is ever achieved without deliberation at The

CODA IN BOLD FACE

Delta. Subscribers are favorably impressed with the sources of almost every item of news in the columns of Dave the Peddler, the state correspondent, and the Mesdames Katharine Hillyer and Katharine Best who conduct "Comstock Vignettes." It all derives from saloons and so must be the true and veritable McCoy. *In vino veritas.*

Three generations of THE ENTERPRISE ago its editors dined magnificently with the nabobs amidst the florid grandeurs of the Washoe Club and lit Jockey Club cigars with the co-owners of everything in sight. To-day's occasions for rejoicing, anniversaries, receptions to visiting notables, and milestones on the highway are observed with double magnums among the prudent thickets of potted palms in the Comstock House or with a whole roast young kid or suckling pig run up at the Delta Restaurant by Four Day Jack Sunara, a chef who has not heard of Gayelord Hauser. Jack refers to the impending entree or relevé as "merchandise." "Look the fine merchandise!" he exclaims, displaying a roasting goat, horns and all, and ready for the oven, among the palsied drinkers at the bar. "Is enough for six," he says with satisfaction. "Weighs thirty pounds."

Visiting editors from shops where there are timeclocks and where sleeping under desks in the daytime is discouraged stroke their chins thoughtfully upon encountering THE ENTERPRISE in its native setting.

As it heads into the home stretch for the century mark as an institution of the West, THE TERRITORIAL ENTERPRISE is Nevada's largest weekly and easily the best-known newspaper in the Silver State. It is, also, by audit of the Audit Bureau of Circulations, the accepted agency of rating for American newspapers, the largest weekly in the Western states of California, Utah, Arizona, Idaho, Colorado, New Mexico, Wyoming, and Montana. It finds itself universally quoted, envied, and in some cases abundantly hated. *Newsweek* remarked of it: "In all the world there isn't a newspaper even remotely resembling THE TERRITORIAL ENTERPRISE."

Its proprietors in the twentieth century are content with this estimate.

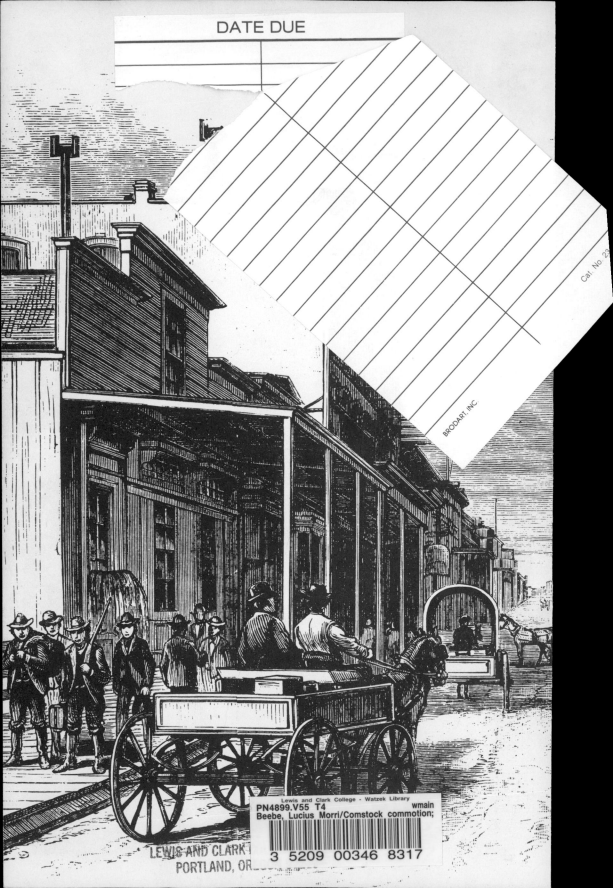